GW00480466

BMW Welt

von der vision zur realität _ from vision to reality

teNeues

Der einzige Realist ist der Visionär. *Federico Fellini (1920-1993, italienischer Regisseur und Schriftsteller)*

The only realist is the visionary. *Federico Fellini (1920-1993, italian director and writer)*

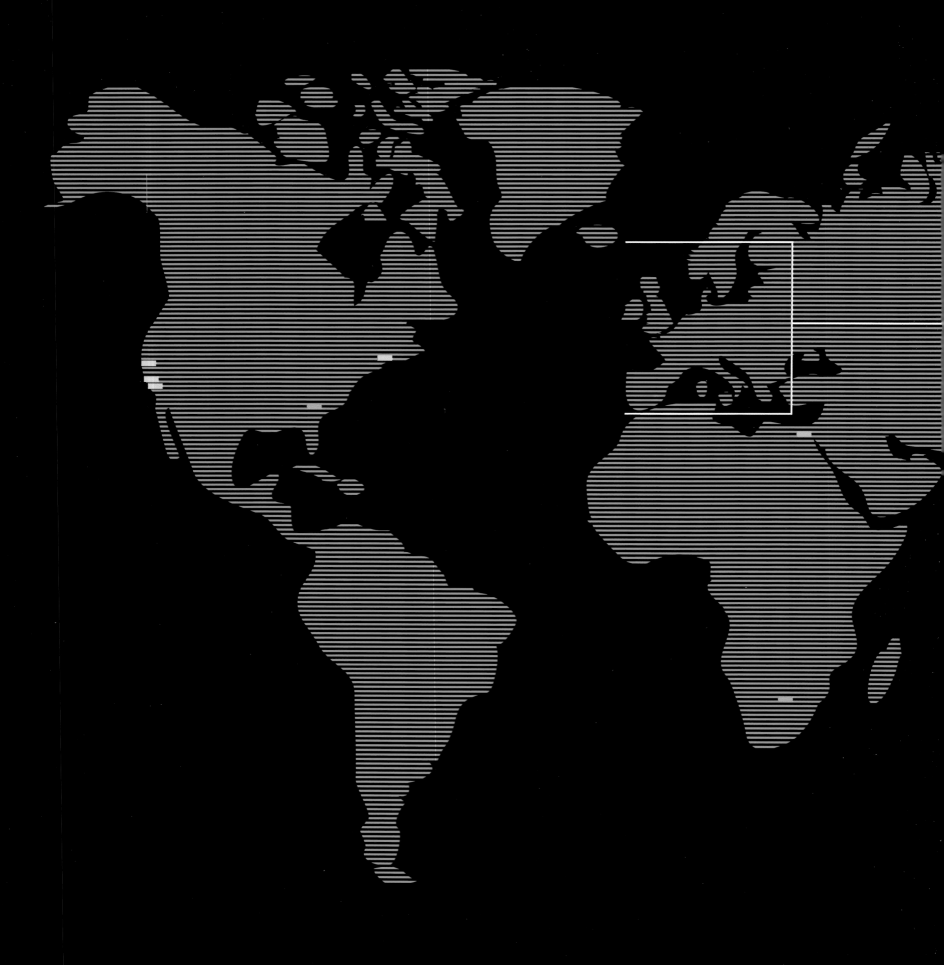

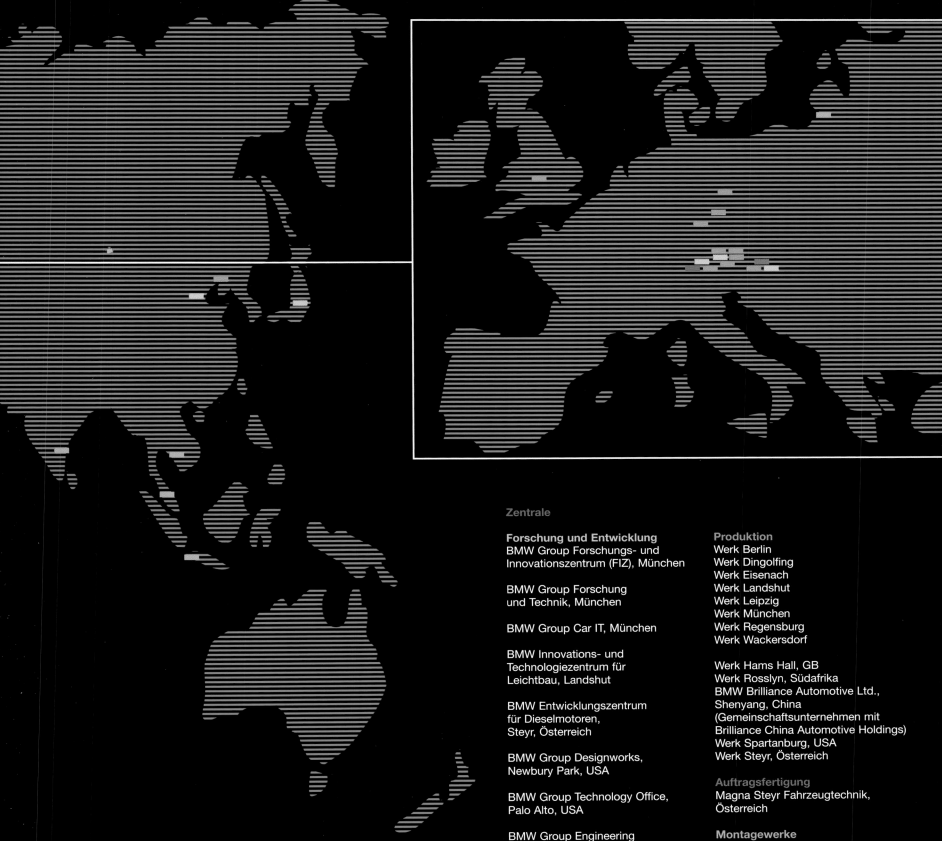

Zentrale

Forschung und Entwicklung
BMW Group Forschungs- und
Innovationszentrum (FIZ), München

BMW Group Forschung
und Technik, München

BMW Group Car IT, München

BMW Innovations- und
Technologiezentrum für
Leichtbau, Landshut

BMW Entwicklungszentrum
für Dieselmotoren,
Steyr, Österreich

BMW Group Designworks,
Newbury Park, USA

BMW Group Technology Office,
Palo Alto, USA

BMW Group Engineering
and Emission Test Center,
Oxnard, USA

BMW Group Technology Office,
Tokio, Japan

BMW Group Entwicklungsbüro,
Peking, China

Produktion
Werk Berlin
Werk Dingolfing
Werk Eisenach
Werk Landshut
Werk Leipzig
Werk München
Werk Regensburg
Werk Wackersdorf

Werk Hams Hall, GB
Werk Rosslyn, Südafrika
BMW Brilliance Automotive Ltd.,
Shenyang, China
(Gemeinschaftsunternehmen mit
Brilliance China Automotive Holdings)
Werk Spartanburg, USA
Werk Steyr, Österreich

Auftragsfertigung
Magna Steyr Fahrzeugtechnik,
Österreich

Montagewerke
Fertigung Chennai, Indien
Fertigung Jakarta, Indonesien
Fertigung Kairo, Ägypten
Fertigung Kaliningrad, Russland
Fertigung Kuala Lumpur, Malaysia
Fertigung Rayong, Thailand

einleitung _ introduction

BMW hat ein weiteres Zeichen gesetzt. Gegenüber dem Olympiapark und in unmittelbarer Nachbarschaft zu Konzernzentrale, Museum und Stammwerk steht das Portal zur Welt von BMW. Die BMW Welt verkörpert die Marke in allen Dimensionen. Sie lässt die Werte, die den Charakter der Marke BMW prägen, erleben. In jedem Augenblick des Aufenthalts vermittelt sie Freude und lässt Leidenschaft, Anspruch und Antrieb der Marke verstehen. Der Auftrag der BMW Welt ist es, die Welt von BMW mit allen Sinnen erlebbar zu machen. In einer emotionalen Architektur wurde ein Ort der Begegnung und der Inspiration geschaffen – offen, abwechslungsreich und involvierend.

BMW has created another impressive landmark: Standing opposite the Olympic Park and in the immediate vicinity of the company's headquarters, museum and home plant, the portal into the world of BMW is to be found. The BMW Welt personifies the brand in all its dimensions. It brings to life the values that characterise the BMW brand's nature. In each and every moment of one's visit it invokes joy and clearly exemplifies the passion, aspirations and the driving force of the brand. It is the mission of the BMW Welt to make the world of BMW a tangible experience for all the senses. Surrounded by emotional architecture, a place for meeting and for inspiration has been created – open, diversified and very engaging.

Seit der Eröffnung der Olympischen Spiele 1972 ist der Olympiapark in München ein attraktives Ziel für Besucher und Stadtbewohner. Unter der zeitlosen Dachkonstruktion aus Plexiglas und Stahl treffen sich seit mehr als 35 Jahren Sportler und Erholungssuchende aus der ganzen Welt. Über 90 Millionen Gäste haben in den Sportarenen der Anlage Wettkämpfe und Spiele, aber auch kulturelle Veranstaltungen besucht. Um die Gebäude herum gliedern Dämme und Wasserläufe die urbane Erlebnislandschaft. In der Mitte erhebt sich der Olympiaturm, seit 1968 eines der Münchner Wahrzeichen und gleichzeitig höchster Aussichtspunkt der Stadt. Die Olympische Anlage ist an 365 Tagen im Jahr mit Leben erfüllt. In erster Linie bildet sie ein riesiges Universum des Sports. Hier ist nicht nur das größte deutsche, athletische Leistungszentrum zu Hause, sondern auch das „Olympic Recreation Centre", in dem das Angebot für Fitness und Gesundheit den Neigungen und Ansprüchen aller Generationen gerecht wird. Wer nicht zum Sport kommt, findet sich bei den vielfältigen Veranstaltungen wieder. Spektakuläre Open-Air-Konzerte oder monumentale Opern, internationale Sommerfestivals sowie bedeutende Ausstellungen und Kongresse finden in den Stadien, den Hallen und auf dem Gelände des Olympiaparks einen passenden Rahmen. Seit der Eröffnung des unterirdisch angelegten Sea Life Centre ist der Olympiapark um eine spannende Attraktion reicher. Ein Park im schönsten Sinne, ein Park für jedermann. Unübersehbare Nachbarn des Olympiaparks waren von Anfang an das Stammwerk und die Konzernzentrale von BMW. Der Wiener Ordinarius für Architektur Prof. Dr. Karl Schwanzer hat das im Volksmund schnell „Vierzylinder" getaufte BMW Hochhaus Ende der 1960er Jahre entworfen. Einer Erzählung nach hatte er vier bayerische Maßkrüge aneinander geschoben und war so auf die Idee zu seinem kleeblattartigen Gebäude gekommen. In Wirklichkeit war es ganz anders: Der Anspruch an optimale Arbeitsbedingungen hatte das moderne Gebäude geformt. Die runde Fassade war eine zwingende Konsequenz, weil ein Kreis im Verhältnis zum Inhalt den kleinsten Umfang hat. Die vierfache Kreisform wurde vom Architekten gewählt, weil sie verglichen mit nur einem Zylinder den Radius der einzelnen Kreise verkleinert. Auch an trüben Tagen bleibt es daher im Inneren des Gebäudes ansprechend hell. Das außergewöhnliche Konstruktionsprinzip des „Vierzylinders" war eine Folge des zeitlich straffen Bauplans. Innerhalb von nur 791 Tagen musste das Gebäude zumindest von außen fertig gestellt werden, um die futuristische Architektur der olympischen Anlage optisch zu bereichern. Anders als bei konventionell errichteten Hochhäusern wurden die 22 Etagen über vier am Gebäudekern befestigte Kragarme erst hydraulisch nach oben gezogen und dann von oben abgehängt. Die Zylinder befinden sich also nicht auf dem Boden, sondern hängen an einem Mittelpylon, der im Inneren des Bauwerkes steht.

Der Architekt des „Vierzylinders" konzipierte zur gleichen Zeit auch das schalenförmige BMW Museum. Beide Gebäude erregten in den frühen 1970er Jahren weltweit Aufsehen und hinterließen deutliche Spuren in der Architekturlandschaft. Bereits damals galt der Gebäudekomplex wegen seiner markanten Form und der ungewöhnlichen Bauweise als Symbol für Fortschritt und Innovation: Architektur, die an die Grenzen des Machbaren führt. Gemeinsam mit dem Olympischen Zeltdach sind sie heute nicht nur Wahrzeichen der bayerischen Landeshauptstadt. Sie gehören zu den Ikonen der Architektur des 20. Jahrhunderts.

Since the opening ceremony of the 1972 Olympic Games, the Olympic Park has been an attractive destination for visitors and the people of Munich. Beneath the timeless roof construction of acrylic glass and steel, sportsmen and women and those seeking recreation or relaxation have been coming here from all around the world for more than 35 years. Over 90 million guests have visited competitions and games but also cultural events in the park's sports arenas. Embankments and watercourses surround the buildings and group the urban recreational landscape together. At the centre, the Olympic Tower punctuates the skyline. Since 1968 it has been one of Munich's prominent landmarks and at the same time it is the city's highest observation platform. The Olympic complex is bustling with activity on 365 days of the year. Primarily, it forms a gigantic world of sports. Not only is the largest competitive athletics centre in Germany at home here, but also the Olympic Recreation Centre, in which the opportunities for fitness and health are tailored to suit the wishes and requirements of young and old alike. Those who seek activities other than sports can enjoy the many varied events. Spectacular open-air concerts or monumental operas, international summer festivals as well as major exhibitions and congresses take place in the appropriate venues of the stadiums, halls and in the grounds of the Olympic Park. Since the opening of the Sea Life Centre in its underground setting, the Olympic Park has been enriched by one further exciting attraction. A park in its loveliest form, a park for everyone. The BMW home plant and the company headquarters have been prominent and quite striking neighbours of the Olympic Park from the very beginning. At the end of the 1960s, Vienna's tenured professor for Architecture, Prof. Dr. Karl Schwanzer, designed the BMW tower, which quickly became commonly known as the "BMW four-cylinder". According to one story, he pushed four Bavarian beer mugs together and thus came up with the idea of the cloverleaf-like high-rise building. In reality it had been quite another story: The requirements for optimum working conditions had shaped this modern building. The circular facades were a coercive consequence, because a circle – in relation to the volume it encloses – has the smallest girth. The fourfold circular form was chosen by the architect because – compared to only a single cylinder – it reduces the radius of the individual circles, and even on overcast days the interior of the building remains agreeably bright. The extraordinary construction principle of the "BMW four-cylinder" was a consequence of the building-plan's strict timetable. Within only 791 days, the building had to be completed, at least from the exterior, in order to optically enrich the futuristic architecture of the Olympic Park complex. In contrast to conventionally constructed high-rise buildings, the 22 storeys were firstly hydraulically lifted up and then hung onto four cantilevers protruding from the building's core. The cylinders therefore are not resting on the ground but are suspended from a central column standing in the building's core.

At the same time, the architect of the "BMW four-cylinder" had also conceived the bowl-shaped BMW Museum building. The construction of both these buildings in the early 1970s caused a worldwide sensation and clearly left its mark in the architectural landscape. Even directly after its construction, the building complex was already considered as a symbol of progress and innovation due to its distinctive form and unusual method of construction: Architecture that pushes the technically feasible to the limit. Together with the Olympic tent-roof, they are today not only landmarks of Bavaria's capital city, but they belong to the icons of 20th century architecture.

Ein weiterer architektonischer und unternehmerischer Meilenstein ist die BMW Welt. Zu Beginn des neuen Jahrtausends setzt das Unternehmen mit diesem Gebäude neue Maßstäbe in der Architektur. Die BMW Welt steht für einen einzigartigen Ort, an dem die Marke vollständig, individuell und überzeugend erlebt werden kann. Mit diesem Projekt entsprach das Unternehmen auch den stetig steigenden Kundenwünschen, ein neues Automobil wieder direkt bei BMW abholen zu können. Für die meisten Menschen ist der Kauf eines Automobils ein Ereignis, das lange geplant und mit Sorgfalt entschieden wird. Denn hier geht es nicht nur um ein Fahrzeug, hier bekommt das Lebensgefühl eine sichtbare Gestalt. Oft beeinflussen eben nicht allein Probefahrten und Hochglanzprospekte die Entscheidung der Käufer. Sie möchten nicht nur ihr neues Fahrzeug, sondern auch die Haltung und das Selbstverständnis einer Marke intensiv kennen lernen. Das Umfeld des neuen Automobils interessiert. Auf welchen Ideen und Innovationen beruht es? Welche Geschichte hat die Marke und mit welchen Technologien arbeitet das Unternehmen? Wo und wie werden die Fahrzeuge produziert? Manche Menschen reisen um die halbe Welt, um Antworten auf diese Fragen zu bekommen. Denn ein Autokauf ist nicht nur eine rationale, sondern auch eine emotionale Entscheidung – das gilt insbesondere für ein BMW Automobil. Die Kunden kommen in die BMW Welt, um „ihre" Marke authentisch zu erleben und begeben sich hier auf eine sinnliche Reise durch die Vergangenheit, Gegenwart und Zukunft der Mobilität. Wie ein Kulminationspunkt fasst die BMW Welt Auslieferungszentrum, Museum und Stammwerk zusammen. Hier wird jeder Gast empfangen, der das Museum besuchen oder die Produktionsstätten im Werk besichtigen möchte. Während im Museum die Entwicklungslinien der Vergangenheit nachgezeichnet werden, erlaubt die Werkführung dem Besucher unmittelbare Einblicke in modernste Produktionsabläufe. Die BMW Welt lädt Kunden, Besucher, Nachbarn, Automobilbegeisterte und Freunde der Marke zum Dialog ein. Themen, die eine innovative Marke wie BMW prägen, werden hier präsentiert und diskutiert. Fragen nach Technik, Design, Mobilität und effizienter Dynamik finden in der BMW Welt eine überzeugende Antwort.

Ungefähr 850.000 Gäste kommen jedes Jahr in das Erlebnis- und Auslieferungszentrum, um die Faszination der Marke kennen zu lernen. Denn das Markenzentrum von BMW an dieser exponierten Stelle ist weitaus mehr als „nur" ein Auslieferungszentrum. Die BMW Welt bietet Raum für Kommunikation und Begegnung. Sie ist ein Forum für Kunst und Kultur, Wissenschaft und Technik, Information und Unterhaltung. Damit ist die BMW Welt nicht nur das Portal zur Marke, sondern auch das Tor, durch das BMW in die Welt hinaus schreitet.

A further architectural and entrepreneurial milestone is the BMW Welt. At the beginning of the new millennium, the company set new standards in architecture with this building. The BMW Welt stands for a worldwide unique place where the brand can be completely, individually and convincingly experienced. With this project the company responded to the increasing desire of the customers to again be able to collect their automobile directly from BMW. For the majority of people, purchasing an automobile is an occasion coupled with much planning and careful decision-making. In such a case it is not only a matter of a vehicle, but one's attitude to life begins to visibly take shape. In fact, test drives and glossy brochures alone are often not enough to influence the buyers' final decision. They want not only their new car, but they also want to intensively get to know the attitude and the self-image of a brand. The environment of the new automobile is intriguing. Upon which ideas and innovations is it based? What is the history of the brand and which technologies does the company employ? Where and how are the vehicles produced? Some people travel halfway around the world to get answers to these questions, because buying a car is not only a rational decision but also an emotional one – and this is especially true of a BMW automobile. The customers come into the BMW Welt to authentically experience "their" brand and enter into a sensual journey through the past, present and future of mobility. Like a point of culmination, the BMW Welt brings together the delivery centre, museum and home plant. Each guest who wants to visit the museum or the production halls in the plant is received here. While the development stages of the past are traced out in the museum, the guided tours through the plant allow the visitor direct insights into the most modern production processes. The BMW Welt invites customers, visitors, neighbours, automobile aficionados and friends of the BMW brand into dialogue. Themes that characterise an innovative brand like BMW are presented here and discussed. Questions about technology, design, mobility and more efficient dynamics receive a convincing response in the BMW Welt.

About 850,000 guests come to the event and delivery centre annually in order to experience the fascination of the brand. Indeed, the brand centre of BMW at this prominent location is considerably more than "just" a delivery centre. The BMW Welt offers space for communication and personal encounters. It is a forum for art and culture, science and technology, information and entertainment. The BMW Welt is therefore not only the portal to the brand, but also the gate through which BMW strides out into the world.

inhaltsverzeichnis _ contents

freude. das portrait einer marke _ joy. portrait of a brand

freude. das portrait einer marke _ joy. portrait of a brand

faszination _ fascination

BMW steht für Freude. Das Verständnis von Freude geht bei BMW weit über das Fahren hinaus. Es ist vielmehr eine grundlegende Einstellung, eine eigene Philosophie und ein Wertesystem, das ein begehrenswertes Lebensgefühl vermittelt. Sportlichkeit und Individualität, Ästhetik und Exklusivität, Leistung und Innovation, Perfektion und Verantwortung sind Charaktermerkmale der Marke. Doch die „Faszination BMW" ist immer mehr als die Summe aller Einzelheiten – weil BMW das Innerste berührt und Emotionen weckt.

BMW stands for joy. At BMW the appreciation of joy reaches far beyond driving itself, it is much more a fundamental attitude, an individual philosophy and a system of values that imparts a desirable awareness of life: Sportsmanship and individuality, aesthetics and exclusiveness, performance and innovation, perfection and responsibility are characteristics of the brand. Indeed, "fascination BMW" is always more than the sum of all individual parts – because BMW touches one's innermost and arouses emotions.

Mit Leidenschaft entwickelt: Sportlich-elegantes Design und innovative Technik definieren die Faszination der Marke. BMW – das ist die Essenz aus Souveränität, Sicherheit und der Freude am Fahren.

Wenn sich irgendwo am Horizont ein winziger Punkt bewegt und langsam an Größe zunimmt, nähert sich da vielleicht ein BMW. Wenn dieser Punkt einmal rechts, dann wieder links im Blickfeld erscheint, ist dieses Fahrzeug vermutlich auf einer kurvenreichen Landstraße und nicht auf der schnurgeraden Autobahn unterwegs. Für den Fahrer ist bereits der Weg das Ziel. Denn er versteht das Fahren nicht nur als Fortbewegung. Er hat Freude daran, die Dynamik und Agilität des Fahrzeuges zu erleben. Weit über eine Million neue Automobile werden bei BMW jedes Jahr produziert. Diese Zahl reflektiert die Begehrlichkeit, die BMW auf der ganzen Welt hervorruft. Schon immer umgibt BMW eine Aura des Besonderen. Aber was ist dieses Besondere? Worauf gründet die „Faszination BMW"? Es ist mehr als nur die verlässliche und innovative Technik, der man sich tagtäglich anvertraut. Es ist das sportlich-elegante Design, das exquisite Interieur und vor allem die Faszination der Fortbewegung. Und aus der Wahrnehmung von Sicherheit und Souveränität, die der Fahrer erlebt, resultiert seine Begeisterung. Es entsteht ein positives Gefühl der Freude!

Nach dem Urteil vieler Experten gehören Fahrzeuge der Marke BMW zu den Besten der Welt. Die Auszeichnungen für Unternehmen und Marke reichen von Bestplatzierungen als beliebtester Arbeitgeber und als Nummer Eins im „Dow Jones Sustainability Index" – einer Unternehmensbewertung, die neben wirtschaftlichen auch soziale und ökologische Aspekte berücksichtigt – bis zum „Gelben Engel" des ADAC für die beste Marke der Welt. 2005 kamen innerhalb eines Jahres weltweit 187 Ehrungen für BMW Automobile zusammen. Und die Liste der Erfolge setzt sich fort: 2007 bekam der BMW 318d ein Öko-Trend-Zertifikat. Die Zeitschrift „Auto Bild" kürte den BMW X5 zum „Wertmeister 2007" und bewertete ihn zusammen mit dem BMW 3er Coupé als beste Neuerscheinung des Jahres. Für BMW EfficientDynamics erhielt BMW das „Grüne Lenkrad". Dennoch ruht sich bei BMW niemand auf den Erfolgen aus. Audi, BMW und Mercedes stehen – in streng alphabetischer Reihenfolge – mit Porsche zusammen im stärksten und gerade deshalb innovativsten Wettbewerb der Welt. Zwei Autostunden voneinander entfernt, ringen diese Marken um die „Pole Position" auf dem Premium-Automobilmarkt. In diesem Prozess hat ein Unternehmen nur dann die besten Chancen, wenn es sich stets neuen sportlichen, wirtschaftlichen, technischen und ökologischen Herausforderungen stellt. Für die Faszination der Marke BMW sind deshalb auch die Mitarbeiter des Unternehmens verantwortlich. Vom Ingenieur bis zum Monteur wagen die Menschen hinter der Marke jeden Tag mit Herz und Verstand das scheinbar Undenk- und Unerreichbare. Es passt zu dieser Philosophie, dass auch die BMW Welt am Anfang eine kühne Vision und ihre Realisierung eine enorme technische und logistische Herausforderung war. Noch vor wenigen Jahren wäre dieses Gebäude ohne die modernen Möglichkeiten der statischen Berechnungen nicht denkbar gewesen. Doch heute wird mit modernster Computertechnik das Unmögliche wahr. Architekten und Bauherr haben sich dieser Aufgabe mit der gleichen Leidenschaft gestellt, mit der auch die Entwicklung fortschrittlichster Produkte bei BMW vorangetrieben wird: Das Bestehende hat seinen Wert – doch das, worum es wirklich geht, ist das Überwinden von Grenzen!

Passionately developed: Sportily elegant design and innovative technology define the fascination of the brand. BMW – its very essence derives from its sovereignty, safety and sheer driving pleasure.

If, somewhere on the horizon a tiny dot is seen to move and slowly grows in size, then perhaps it's a BMW approaching. If the dot suddenly appears in view to the left and then to the right, then presumably the vehicle is on a serpentine country road and not moving along a dead straight highway. For the driver, the journey has already become the reward, because he considers driving not simply to be a means of transportation and takes pleasure in experiencing the dynamics and the agility of the vehicle. Far more than a million new automobiles are produced by BMW each year. Such a volume defines the desire that BMW evokes all around the world. BMW has always been surrounded by an aura of the exceptional. Although, what is exceptional? What is "fascination BMW" based on? It is more than just the reliable and innovative technology that one confides in every day. It is the sportily-elegant design, the exquisite interior, the well engineered and innovative technology, and above all the fascination of locomotion. And from the experience of security and sovereignty, there arises a sense of enthusiasm, a positive feeling of joy.

In the opinion of many experts vehicles of the BMW brand belong to the best in the world. The awards for the company and its brand range from first places as most popular employer and as number one in the "Dow Jones Sustainability Index" – a business appraisal that takes economic as well as social and ecological aspects into account – to the "Gelber Engel" award of the German automobile association ADAC for the best brand in the world. Within 2005 alone, the company accumulated worldwide 187 honours for BMW automobiles. And the list of successes continues: In 2007, the BMW 318d received an "Automobile Environment Certificate" from the Öko-Trend Institute. The magazine "Auto Bild" voted the BMW X5 "Wertmeister 2007" and rated it together with the BMW 3 Series Coupé as the best new release of the year. For BMW EfficientDynamics, BMW received the "Grünes Lenkrad" award. Nevertheless, not for a minute does anyone at BMW bask in their successes. Audi, BMW and Mercedes stand – in strictly alphabetical order – together with Porsche in the toughest and, particularly for this reason, most innovative competition in the world. Two hours' drive from each other, these brands contend for pole position in the market for premium automobiles. In this process, a company only then has the best chances if it continually takes up new sporting, economic, technical and ecological challenges. Therefore also the employees have responsibility for the fascination of the BMW brand. From engineer to assembly operator, the people behind the brand dare to challenge the apparently unthinkable and seemingly unattainable each day with conviction and competence. It is also fitting to this philosophy that the BMW Welt was a daring vision as well, and its later realisation was an enormous technical and logistic challenge. Until only a few years ago, this building would have been unthinkable without the modern possibilities of calculations of its statics. However, today the impossible becomes reality with cutting-edge computer technology. Architects and client met this challenge with equal fervour, with which also the development of the most progressive products at BMW are further promoted: What is established has its intrinsic value – but that which is of essential consequence, is the overcoming of limitations!

herkunft _ origins

BMW befand sich schon immer in Bewegung, entwickelte sich ständig weiter und ist bis heute geprägt durch Innovationskraft und Zielstrebigkeit. Am Anfang standen nicht Motorräder oder Automobile, sondern Motoren für die Flugzeugindustrie. Mitten im Ersten Weltkrieg ging die BMW GmbH am 21. Juli 1917 aus den Rapp Motorenwerken hervor. Das Unternehmen BMW war geboren und mit ihm das weiß-blaue Firmenemblem, das heute weltweit für effiziente Dynamik, innovative Technologie und individuelle Exklusivität steht.

BMW has always been on the move, continually evolving, and to this day it is characterised by innovative energy and determination. In the beginning, neither motorcycles nor automobiles were manufactured, but engines for the aviation industry. In the middle of the First World War, BMW GmbH emerged from Rapp Motorenwerke on 21st July 1917. Thus, as a company, BMW was born, and with it the blue and white company emblem, which today stands for efficient dynamics, innovative technologies and individual exclusiveness worldwide.

Das Oberwiesenfeld – ein zentraler Ort: Am Standort des Stammwerks (1920) flog Franz Zeno Diemer 1919 den ersten Höhenweltrekord für BMW. Auch der Rennfahrer Ernst Jakob Henne war hier am Flughafen mit seiner BMW R4 anzutreffen (1935).

Am Oberwiesenfeld im Norden von München begann die Historie von BMW. Hier, in unmittelbarer Nähe der BMW Welt liegt noch heute das Stammwerk der BMW AG. Schon die ersten Produkte, Flugmotoren, zeichneten sich durch ihre überdurchschnittliche Qualität und Leistungsstärke in großen Höhen aus. Am 17. Juni 1919 erreichte der Testpilot Franz Zeno Diemer mit seiner DFW IV, angetrieben von einem BMW IV Motor, erstmals eine Flughöhe von 9.760 Metern. Eine bahnbrechende und die erste in einer langen Reihe von Höchst- und Erstleistungen für BMW in der Luft. Doch BMW konnte auf diesem Erfolg nicht aufbauen. Der Versailler Vertrag untersagte Deutschland unter anderem auch die Produktion von Flugmotoren. Alle Anlagen zum Flugmotorenbau mussten zerstört werden. BMW fertigte stattdessen nach einer Lizenz der Knorr-Bremse AG Eisenbahnbremsen und Einbaumotoren. 1922 verkaufte das Unternehmen den Motorenbau mit dem Namen BMW an die 1916 gegründeten Bayerischen Flugzeugwerke (BFW) und zog in deren Werkhallen in der Lerchenauer Straße, dem heutigen BMW Stammwerk, um. Camillo Castiglioni hieß der neue Eigentümer, der den Namen, das Emblem, die Patente, die Schutzrechte, Zeichnungen und Entwürfe kaufte.

Das Jahr 1923 brachte gleich zwei Veränderungen für die BMW AG: Die Alliierten erlaubten die eingeschränkte Wiederaufnahme der Flugmotorenproduktion. Außerdem entwickelte sich aus der Fertigung von Stationär- und Einbauaggregaten für unterschiedliche Verwendungszwecke ein zweites Standbein des jungen Unternehmens: Die BMW Ingenieure konstruierten um den „Bayern-Kleinmotor" herum ein eigenes Motorrad – die R32. Sie war das erste Fahrzeug mit BMW Markenzeichen auf den Straßen. Ebenso wie die BMW Flugmotoren standen auch die Motorräder des Münchner Unternehmens für hohe Qualität, technischen Fortschritt, Zuverlässigkeit und Sportlichkeit, wie zahlreiche Rennsportsiege und Rekorde belegen. So stellte Ernst Jakob Henne auf BMW Maschinen zwischen 1929 und 1937 insgesamt 76 Geschwindigkeitsrekorde auf. Am 28.11.1937 erreichte er auf einem BMW Motorrad 279,5 km/h und stellte damit einen Rekord auf, der bis 1951 halten sollte. So gelang es BMW, den Wettlauf um das schnellste Motorrad der Welt für sich zu entscheiden. Auf Rennsportveranstaltungen wie der Internationalen Sechstagefahrt oder der Tourist Trophy auf der Isle of Man konnten immer wieder Fahrer auf BMW Motorrädern den Sieg erringen. Auch nach 1945 waren sie äußerst erfolgreich. 1954 wurde ein BMW Seitenwagen-Gespann Team-Weltmeister. Mit diesem WM-Titel begann eine im Rennsport einmalige Erfolgsserie. Bis 1974 gewann BMW insgesamt 19 Fahrer- und 20 Markenweltmeisterschaften. Nach der teilweisen Revision des Versailler Vertrages öffnete sich erneut die Tür für die Flugmotorenproduktion, die bis 1945 das wichtigste Betätigungsfeld der BMW AG bleiben sollte. Die Hauptabnehmermärkte waren zunächst die Sowjetunion, die Tschechoslowakei und Japan. Die Luftfahrt der Zwischenkriegszeit zeichnete sich durch eine kontinuierliche Weiterentwicklung der Flugzeuge aus, die nach Antrieben mit großer Leistung und dauerhafter Betriebssicherheit verlangten. Statt neue kostenintensive Konzepte zu verfolgen, bemühten sich die Ingenieure von BMW, die bereits bewährten Baumuster weiterzuentwickeln. 1928 schuf sich BMW mit dem Kauf der Fahrzeugfabrik Eisenach ein drittes Standbein: die Automobilproduktion. Zunächst produzierte BMW in Thüringen den BMW 3/15 PS, der auf einer Lizenz des Austin Seven basierte. Das erste selbst entwickelte

The Oberwiesenfeld – a central location: At the same place as the home plant (1920), Franz Zeno Diemer flew the first altitude world record for BMW in 1919. The motorcycle road racer Ernst Jakob Henne was also to be seen here at the airfield with his BMW R4 (1935).

At Oberwiesenfeld in North Munich the history of BMW began. The home plant of BMW AG is still situated here in the immediate vicinity of the BMW Welt. It was already apparent with the first products, aircraft engines, that they stood out through their superior quality and high-performance at high altitude. On 17th June 1919, the test pilot Franz Zeno Diemer attained an altitude of 32,000ft (9,760m) for the first time with his DFW IV, powered by a BMW IV engine. It was a pioneering achievement and the first in a long line of highest and first achievements for BMW in the air. However, BMW was unable to expand upon this success. The Treaty of Versailles forbade Germany to produce, among other things, aircraft engines. All facilities for the construction of aircraft engines had to be destroyed. Instead, BMW manufactured railway brake systems and built-in engines under licence from Knorr-Bremse AG. In 1922 the company sold its engine manufacture together with the BMW name to the Bayerische Flugzeugwerke (BFW) that was founded in 1916, and moved into their factory workshops in Lerchenauer Strasse, today's BMW home plant. Camillo Castiglioni was the new owner who bought the company's name, emblem, patents, property rights, drawings and draft designs.

In the year 1923 two important changes occurred for BMW AG: The Entente Powers allowed limited resumption of aircraft engine production. In addition to this, the young company developed a second string to its bow through the assembly of stationary and built-in units for various purposes: BMW engineers constructed their own motorcycle based around the "Bayern-Kleinmotor" (Bavarian small engine) – the R32. It was the first vehicle with the BMW brand name for general road use. Just like the BMW aircraft engines, the motorcycles of the Munich company stood for high quality, technical improvement, reliability and sportiness, which numerous motor racing victories and records attest. Thus, Ernst Jakob Henne achieved a total of 76 speed records on BMW motorcycles between 1929 and 1937. Again on a BMW motorcycle on 28th November 1937, he reached 173.5 mph (279.5 km/h) and set a record that was to hold until 1951. BMW was thereby successful in winning the race to develop the world's fastest motorcycle. At racing events such as the International Six Day Trial or the Tourist Trophy on the Isle of Man, competitors on BMW motorcycles were able time and again to achieve victories. Also after 1945, they were very successful, and a BMW side-car team became world champion in 1954. With this world championship title, a unique series of racing successes began. Up to 1974, BMW had won a total of 19 riders' and 20 manufacturers' championships. The partial revision of the Versailles Treaty once again opened the way for the production of aircraft engines, which was to remain the most important activity of BMW AG up to 1945. Initially, the principal markets were the Soviet Union, Czechoslovakia and Japan. Aviation in the inter-war years was distinguished by a continual further development of aircraft, which demanded power plants with ever-greater performance and durable operational safety. Instead of pursuing costly new developments, the engineers at BMW strove to further develop the already proven construction designs. With the acquisition of the Eisenach automobile factory in 1928, BMW created for itself a third manufacturing foothold: automobile production. Here in Thuringia, BMW initially produced the BMW 3/15 PS that was based on an Austin Seven licence. The first self-developed automobile came onto the market in 1932 as the BMW 3/20 PS. The technologically

Neuanfang nach dem Zweiten Weltkrieg: Nach kurzer Aufbauphase startete BMW 1948 mit dem Motorrad R24 in die Nachkriegszeit. Ab den 1950er Jahren ergänzten Luxusautomobile wie der BMW 501 sowie das Motocoupé Isetta das Programm.

Automobil kam 1932 mit dem BMW 3/20 PS auf den Markt. Ein Jahr später folgte der technologisch ehrgeizige BMW 303. Ausgestattet mit dem fortschrittlichen Motorkonzept des Reihensechszylinders zeigte der Kühlergrill des Fahrzeuges zum ersten Mal die bis heute charakteristische BMW Niere. Zur Automobilbegeisterung gehörte auch der Motorsport. Er wurde zum entscheidenden Werbeträger mit dem Sieg des BMW Teams beim Alpenpokal 1929 und bei der Rallye Monte Carlo 1930. Diese sportlichen Erfolge machten BMW international bekannt. Automobile Mythen entstanden, wie der legendäre Sportwagen 328 von 1937, der zwar nur 464 Mal gebaut wurde, dessen Siege jedoch entscheidend zum Image der Marke BMW beigetragen haben. Im Zuge der nationalsozialistischen Rüstungspolitik wandelte sich BMW immer stärker zu einem Rüstungsunternehmen und forcierte die Produktion von Flugmotoren. Nach dem Beginn des Zweiten Weltkrieges wurde die zivile Produktion von Automobilen und Motorrädern eingestellt. Nach Kriegsende 1945 waren die Fabrikanlagen schließlich zerstört oder wurden von den Siegermächten demontiert. Das Werk Eisenach im sowjetisch verwalteten Sektor Deutschlands konnte nicht mehr genutzt werden und war damit ebenfalls für BMW verloren.

Für BMW begann die Nachkriegszeit zunächst mit der Notproduktion von Haushaltsgeräten sowie der Einrichtung einer Reparaturwerkstatt. 1948 produzierte BMW mit der R24 zunächst wieder Motorräder. Drei Jahre später nahm das Unternehmen die Automobilproduktion auf. Doch weder der „Barockengel" BMW 501, der als Einsatzfahrzeug der bayerischen Polizei in der TV-Serie „Isar 12" zum Fernsehstar avancierte, noch seine Nachfolger konnten die notwendigen Verkaufszahlen erreichen. Kleinere, bezahlbare Autos wurden zum Symbol für den wirtschaftlichen wie auch mobilen Aufschwung in Deutschland. Mit der in Lizenz produzierten Isetta traf BMW hingegen den Zeitgeist der 1950er Jahre und stillte auch die Sehnsucht kleiner Leute nach Mobilität. Mehr als 160.000 Modelle dieses Kleinstwagens wurden zwischen 1955 und 1962 verkauft. Dennoch reichte der Erfolg der Isetta nicht aus, um wirtschaftliche Gewinne zu erzielen. Gleichzeitig war das Motorradgeschäft seit Mitte der 1950er Jahre rückläufig. Das alleine wäre keine Bedrohung für das Unternehmen gewesen. Doch seit der Produktionsaufnahme schrieb die Automobilsparte rote Zahlen. Der Grund war ein unausgewogenes Programm, in dem zwischen V8-Limousinen und Kleinstwagen eine große Lücke klaffte. So geriet BMW Ende der 1950er Jahre in eine existenzbedrohende Krise. Der Verkauf des Unternehmens war im Dezember 1959 beschlossene Sache. Doch nun zeigte sich die emotionale Stärke der Marke. Händler und Kleinaktionäre stemmten sich erfolgreich gegen einen Verkauf. Mit Herbert Quandt bekam BMW einen neuen Großaktionär, der sein Vertrauen in das Unternehmen, seine Marke und den BMW 700 setzte – einen Kleinwagen, für den bereits viele Bestellungen vorlagen und der in den ersten Jahren die Hauptlast der Sanierung tragen sollte. So blieb BMW eigenständig und der Erfolg, der in den 1960er Jahren seinen Anfang nahm, belegte die weitsichtige Entscheidung Quandts. Er und die BMW Manager erkannten, dass man die Kraft der Marke nutzen musste. BMW hatte aus seinen Fehlern und Krisen gelernt und berücksichtigte zum ersten Mal nach dem Krieg gesellschaftliche und demographische Aspekte bei der Vermarktung seiner Automobile. Mit dem BMW 1500, dem ersten Modell der „Neuen Klasse", startete das Unternehmen 1962 in eine Phase der Modellpolitik, die den Zeitgeschmack traf: sportlich, elegant,

New beginnings after the Second World War: After a short period of reestablishment, BMW began its post-war phase in 1948 with the R24 motorcycle. From the 1950s, luxury automobiles such as the BMW 501 as well as the Motocoupé Isetta supplemented the range.

ambitious BMW 303 followed a year later. Equipped with the advanced engine concept of the straight-six-cylinder, the vehicle's radiator grill displayed for the first time the characteristic "BMW kidney" form still used today. Motor racing was already part of general automobile enthusiasm and it became a decisive advertising medium with the victory of the BMW team at the Alpine Cup in 1929 and at the Monte Carlo Rally in 1930. These motor sport successes made BMW internationally known. Automobile myths arose, such as the legendary 328 sports car from 1937 that had a production run of only 464 units, but its victories however had decisively contributed to the image of the BMW brand. Within the framework of Hitler's national socialist armaments policies, BMW evolved ever more strongly into an armaments manufacturer, forcing the production of aircraft engines. After the beginning of the Second World War, non-military production of automobiles and motorcycles was suspended. After war's end in 1945, the plants were ultimately destroyed or were dismantled by the allied powers. The Eisenach plant in the Soviet controlled sector of Germany could no longer be used and thereby also became a total loss for BMW.

For BMW the post-war period initially began with emergency production of household appliances as well as the establishment of repair workshops. In 1948, BMW once again produced motorcycles to begin with, the first of which was the R24. Three years later the company again began automobile production. However, neither the "Baroque Angel" BMW 501 – that became a star as a police car in the TV series "Isar 12" – nor its successor was able to attain the necessary sales levels. Smaller, affordable cars became the symbol for the economic as well as the mobility boom in Germany. On the other hand, with the Isetta, produced under licence, BMW hit upon the zeitgeist of the 1950s and satisfied the yearning of ordinary people for mobility. More than 160,000 models of this tiny car were sold between 1955 and 1962. Nevertheless, the success of the Isetta was not sufficient to reap economic gains. At the same time, the motorcycle business had been declining since the middle of the 1950s. In itself, it would not have been a threat to the company, but automobile production had been operating in the red since its re-commencement. The reason was an unbalanced production programme, in which there was a yawning gap between V8 limousines and small cars. Thus, at the end of the 1950s, BMW was moving into a crisis that threatened its existence. In December 1959, the sale of the company had already been decided. However, now the emotional strength of the brand became apparent. Dealers and small shareholders successfully consolidated themselves against selling the company. BMW received a new major shareholder in the shape of Herbert Quandt, who placed his confidence in the company, in its brand and in the BMW 700 – a small car for which many orders had already been taken and which was to carry the main burden of the restructuring changes. Thus, BMW remained independent and the success that had its beginnings in the 1960s confirmed Quandt's far-sighted decision. He and the BMW managers recognised that the power of the brand needed to be utilised. BMW had learned from its mistakes and crises, and for the first time after the war had taken into account societal and demographic aspects for the marketing of its automobiles. In 1962, with the BMW 1500, the first model of the "New Class", the company started to build models that hit the fashion of the

Eine neue Generation: In den 1970er Jahren entwickelte BMW eine einheitliche und konsequente Bezeichnung der Baureihen, die bis heute Gültigkeit hat. Als erstes Produkt wurde 1972 der BMW 5er eingeführt. 1975 und 1977 folgten die ersten BMW 3er und BMW 7er.

technisch innovativ und qualitativ hochwertig. Die Nachfrage war überwältigend und läutete für das Unternehmen eine lang andauernde Erfolgsgeschichte ein. 1963 schrieb das Unternehmen wieder schwarze Zahlen. Die Modelle der „Neuen Klasse" und die seit Mitte der 1960er Jahre produzierte 02-Serie waren so erfolgreich, dass BMW auch wieder größere Limousinen und Coupés ins Programm nahm. Sportlich-kompakte und leistungsstarke Automobile wurden zum Charaktermerkmal der Marke. Die Produktpalette hatte sich so stark vergrößert, dass die Produktionskapazitäten in München nicht mehr ausreichten. 1967 kaufte BMW die Hans Glas GmbH in Dingolfing. Hier entstand das bis heute größte Werk, in dem seit 1973 die 5er-Reihe und seit 1977 die 7er-Reihe vom Band läuft. Mehr als 20.000 Menschen bauen dort heute täglich bis zu 1.300 Fahrzeuge der verschiedensten Modellreihen. 1975 löste die 3er Reihe die „02er-Reihe" ab und entwickelte sich zur erfolgreichsten Modellreihe des Unternehmens. Mut zahlte sich aus. Im Olympiajahr 1972 befand sich das Unternehmen weiter ungebremst auf Wachstumskurs. Mit Eberhard von Kuenheim an der Spitze verbuchte BMW in dieser Zeit einen Erfolg nach dem anderen. Es war die Ära eines erfolgreich handelnden Unternehmers, die 23 Jahre dauern und in der eine Vielzahl von Baureihen und Modellen auf den Weg gebracht werden sollte. Unter von Kuenheims Führung wurde das Unternehmen in den 1970er Jahren endgültig zu einem international agierenden Konzern. Ein klar profiliertes Modellprogramm aus 3er-, 5er- und 7er-Reihe entstand. 1987 entwickelte BMW erstmals wieder nach dem Krieg einen 12-Zylinder und etablierte sich damit an der Weltspitze der Automobilindustrie. Mit dem Kauf der britischen Rover Group kam das Unternehmen in den 1990er Jahren kurzfristig vom Erfolgskurs ab. Die Unternehmensspitze entschied sich dann aber für eine klare Konzentration auf ein Programm von Premium-Fahrzeugen, so dass vom britischen Konzernteil nur die Marke MINI in der BMW Group verblieb. Später wurde zudem Rolls-Royce Motor Cars in das Markenportfolio integriert. BMW konzentrierte sich wieder auf seine Kernwerte und seine starke Herkunft. Das war keine Kapitulation, sondern eine strategische Grundsatzentscheidung. Das Unternehmen organisierte sich neu und der Startschuss für einen neuen, kleineren BMW fiel: die 1er-Reihe. Wieder einmal hatte BMW die Hand am Puls der Zeit. Mit der Erkenntnis, dass ein Premium-Automobil auch kompakt sein kann. Vorausgesetzt, die unverwechselbare „Freude am Fahren" bleibt.

Die Historie der BMW Automobile und Motorräder ist geprägt vom unablässigen Streben nach innovativen Produkten, die den Geist der „Freude am Fahren" transportieren. 328, 507, 700, 1800, 2002, M1 – diese historischen Automobile prägen bis heute nachhaltig den Mythos BMW. Im BMW Museum wird die Geschichte des Unternehmens zum Erlebnis. Seit der Eröffnung 1973 wird hier neben bedeutenden Exponaten die Entwicklung des Unternehmens BMW anschaulich dargestellt. Doch im Laufe der Jahre wurde die „Museumsschüssel" mit rund 1.000 Quadratmetern Ausstellungsfläche schließlich zu klein. Der Bau der BMW Welt und die gleichzeitige Sanierung der Konzernzentrale war der passende Moment, um das Museum neu auszurichten und deutlich zu vergrößern. Das mittlerweile denkmalgeschützte Gebäude wurde außen erhalten, innen aber völlig entkernt. Hier und im Flachbau zwischen Hochhaus und BMW Welt entstand auf mehreren Ebenen ein völlig neu konzipiertes Museum.

A new generation: In the 1970s, BMW developed uniform and consistent designations for the model ranges that are valid to this day. The BMW 5 Series was introduced in 1972 as the first of these products. The first BMW 3 Series and BMW 7 Series followed in 1975 and 1977.

times: sporty, elegant, technically innovative and qualitatively high-grade. The demand was overwhelming and heralded for the company the start of a long-lasting success story. By 1963 the company was once again in the black. From the mid-1960s, the models of the "New Class" and the 02 Series were so popular that BMW re-introduced larger sedans and coupés into their programme. Sportily compact and high-performance automobiles became characteristic of the BMW brand. The product range had now expanded so much that production capacities in Munich were no longer adequate. In 1967, BMW bought Hans Glas GmbH in Dingolfing, and it was here that BMW's largest plant to date was to emerge, in which since 1973 the 5 Series – and since 1977 the 7 Series – rolled off the line. Here, more than 20,000 people daily produce up to 1,300 vehicles of various model ranges. The 3 Series replaced the 02 Series in 1975 and it developed into the company's most successful model range. Audacity had paid off. In the Olympic year of 1972, the company was to find itself once again in further unchecked expansion. With Eberhard von Kuenheim at the top, BMW reported one success after another in this period. It was the era of a successfully operating entrepreneur that was to last 23 years and in which a variety of ranges and models were to be put into production. Under his leadership, BMW definitively became an internationally operational company in the 1970s. A clearly profiled programme of models emerged from the 3, 5 and 7 Series. In 1987, for the first time after the war, BMW developed a 12-cylinder, thereby establishing itself as a world-leader in the automobile industry. With the acquisition of Britain's Rover Group, the company briefly strayed from its successful course during the 1990s. The BMW leadership then however decided upon a clear concentration on a programme of premium vehicles, so that from the company's British sector only the MINI brand remained in the BMW Group. Later on, Rolls-Royce Motor Cars was also integrated into the company's portfolio of brands. BMW concentrated once again on its core values and its strong heritage. This was in no way a capitulation, but rather a strategic policy decision. The company re-organised itself anew and the starting signal for a new, smaller BMW was given: the 1 Series. Once again, BMW had a firm grip on the pulse of the times with the realisation that a premium automobile can also be compact, provided that the unmistakeable "sheer driving pleasure" firmly remains.

The history of BMW automobiles and motorcycles is characterised by the relentless pursuit for innovative products that convey the spirit of "sheer driving pleasure". The 328, 507, 700, 1800, 2002 and the M1 – these historic automobiles still continue to lastingly characterise the BMW legend. In the BMW Museum, the history of the company becomes an impressive experience. Since its opening in 1973 and alongside significant exhibits, the development of BMW as a company is vividly displayed. However, over the years the characteristic bowl-shaped building, with approximately 1,000 square metres of exhibition area, had ultimately become too small. The construction of the BMW Welt and the concurrent renovation of the company's headquarters was the perfect moment to reorganise the museum and to significantly enlarge it. The building, which has meanwhile been listed on the historic register, has had its exterior preserved but its interior has been completely gutted. Here and in the low-rise building between the tower and the BMW Welt, a fully re-designed multi-level museum has emerged.

können _ expertise

Schnelligkeit ist längst nicht mehr das wichtigste Charaktermerkmal eines Automobils. In einer Welt, in der Mobilität zu den Grundvoraussetzungen unserer Gesellschaft gehört, ist verantwortungsvolles und nachhaltiges Handeln entscheidend. Dies bedeutet für BMW nicht nur, Kunden bessere Fahrleistungen bei weniger Verbrauch und mit geringeren Emissionen zu bieten. Es bedeutet auch, Prozesse schneller zu gestalten, die Organisation flexibler auszurichten und die Suche nach der besten Lösung nie aufzugeben.

For some time now, speed has ceased to be the most important characteristic of an automobile. In a world in which mobility is one of the basic prerequisites of society, responsible and sustainable transactions are decisive. For BMW this means offering the customer not only better driving performance with more efficiency and lower emissions, but it also means reorganising processes to be faster, adapting the organisation to be more flexible and never to give up the search for the best solution.

Visionäre Entwürfe: Die innovativen Gebäude von BMW Museum,
BMW Stammwerk und „Vierzylinder" setzen durch ihre
starke architektonische Außenwirkung weithin sichtbare Zeichen.

Welche Anforderungen ein Automobil der Extraklasse heute erfüllen muss, hat Eberhard von Kuenheim bereits 1993 auf dem „Automotive News World Congress" in Detroit formuliert. Er sprach nicht nur von der außergewöhnlichen Leistung, sondern auch von einer besonderen Verantwortung der Automobilindustrie, nicht zuletzt für die Ökologie: „In Staus vergeuden wir volkswirtschaftliche Leistung und Energie und wir belasten unsere Umwelt. Massenhafte Mobilität behindert die Beweglichkeit von Wirtschaft und Staat. Wir haben alle die Botschaft verstanden, dass wir nicht ungebremst Energie vergeuden dürfen. Gute Organisation allein löst diese Aufgaben nicht", sagte von Kuenheim. „Was wir benötigen, ist wiederum Mobilität, geistige Mobilität. Sie bedeutet, mit dem Erreichten niemals zufrieden zu sein, den Kopf frei zu halten und frei zu sein für Neues. Es heißt, sein Ingenium zu entwickeln. Der Beruf des Ingenieurs nutzt dieses Wort. ‚Engineering' ist daher weit mehr als der Umgang mit Masse und Energie. Es ist der Umgang mit Ideen."

BMW hat neben der Umsetzung technischer und ökonomischer Konzepte auch ökologische Ziele definiert und erreicht. So hat das Unternehmen als einer der ersten Automobilhersteller funktionierende Konzepte für das Recycling von Fahrzeugen erarbeitet und eingeführt. Mit Weitblick wurde schon Anfang der 1990er Jahre die Vision von nachhaltigem Handeln, vernetzter Mobilität und intelligenten Verkehrssystemen entworfen. Eine Haltung, die heute Alltag geworden ist. BMW sieht in diesem visionären Geist einen Grund für seine vorherrschende Marktposition. Kennzeichnend für das Unternehmen ist zugleich die Bereitschaft und Fähigkeit, mehr kalkulierbare Risiken als andere einzugehen. Über Jahrzehnte hinweg hat BMW bei der Entwicklung neuer Produkte nicht nur auf bewährte Technik gesetzt. Innovative Technologien aus dem Motorsport wurden erfolgreich in den automobilen Alltag übernommen. Auch die wirtschaftliche Risikobereitschaft zahlte sich aus, wie die Finanzierung des Unternehmens durch Herbert Quandt Ende der 1950er Jahre gezeigt hat. Innerhalb der letzten 40 Jahre hat BMW seine Produktion um das Neunfache, den Umsatz um das 60-fache und den Ertrag sogar um das 140-fache gesteigert. Mitten in der ersten Ölpreiskrise der 1970er Jahre eröffnete BMW das heute größte Werk im niederbayerischen Dingolfing. In den 1980er Jahren entstanden zwei Drittel der neuen Arbeitsplätze in der gesamten deutschen Automobilindustrie bei BMW. 1967 wurde das Montagewerk in Rosslyn, Südafrika, übernommen. Hier setzte sich das Unternehmen für eine weitgehende Gleichberechtigung der Mitarbeiter aller Hautfarben innerhalb der Werkmauern ein. Kurz nachdem Volkswagen seine USA-Fabrik schließen musste, baute BMW in den USA seine Produktion auf – ein kontrolliertes Wagnis, das sich als lohnend erwies. In Regensburg trennte der Konzern Maschinenlaufzeiten und individuelle Arbeitszeiten voneinander – ein Modell, das im Werk Leipzig konsequent fortgesetzt wurde und beispielhaft für eine effektive, soziale und global wettbewerbsfähige Produktion werden sollte. In einer Zeit, in der viele Unternehmen ihre Produktionsstätten ins Ausland verlagerten, beschritt BMW damit einen Erfolg versprechenden Weg, um die wirtschaftliche Bedeutung des Standortes Deutschland zu erhalten. BMW ist heute führend auf dem Sektor der individuellen Mobilität. Die Kernbotschaft wird über den Markenslogan transportiert: „Freude am Fahren". Diese Aussage impliziert die schönste und wichtigste Herausforderung, technisch und ästhetisch überzeugende Automobile zu entwickeln

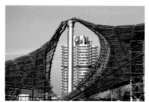

Visionary concepts: The innovative buildings of the BMW Museum, the BMW home plant and the "BMW four-cylinder" set visibly far reaching examples through their stark architectural public image.

The requirements that a vehicle in a class of its own needs to fulfil, had already been formulated by Eberhard von Kuenheim at the "Automotive News World Congress" in Detroit in 1993. He spoke not only of the automobile industry and its remarkable achievements, but also of the automobile industry's special responsibility, not least for ecology: "We waste economic performance and energy due to traffic congestion and we put a strain on our environment. Mobility on a massive scale overburdens the mobility of the economy and of the state. We have all understood the message that we are not allowed to unrestrictedly waste energy. Good organisation alone does not solve these duties", said von Kuenheim. "What we require is in turn mobility, mental mobility. This means never being satisfied with that which has been achieved, to retain an open mind and to be open for innovations. This also means developing one's genius. The engineer's profession utilises this word, and 'engineering' is therefore much more than dealing with mass and energy. It also entails dealing with ideas."

Along with the implementation of technical and economic concepts, BMW has also defined and achieved ecological aims. Thus, as one of the first automobile manufacturers, the company has developed and introduced functioning concepts for the recycling of vehicles. With farsightedness, as early as the beginning of the 1990s, the vision of sustainable transactions, networked mobility and intelligent traffic systems was conceived. An attitude that has today become everyday practice. In this visionary spirit, BMW also sees a reason for its dominant market position. At the same time, the readiness and ability to run more calculated risks than others is typical for the company. For decades BMW has relied not only on proven technologies in their development of new products. Innovative motor racing technologies were successfully employed in the everyday automobile world. Furthermore, the economic readiness to take risks paid off, as is demonstrated by the financing of the company through Herbert Quandt at the end of the 1950s. Within the last 40 years BMW has increased its production 9-fold, its turnover 60-fold and its returns by as much as 140-fold. At the height of the first oil crisis in the 1970s, BMW opened a new plant in Dingolfing in Lower Bavaria that is today its largest. In the 1980s, two thirds of new jobs in the entire German automobile industry arose at BMW. In 1967 the assembly plant in Rosslyn, South Africa was taken over. Here the company significantly promoted equality for all employees within the premises, regardless of ethnic origin. Shortly after Volkswagen had to close its US factory, BMW established its production in the USA – a controlled risk, which proved to be appropriate and successful. In Regensburg, Germany, the BMW group separated machinery uptimes and individual working hours from one another – a model that was consistently followed up in the Leipzig plant and that should prove to be exemplary for an effective, social and globally competitive production. At a time in which many companies were relocating their production plants abroad, BMW thereby set out on a path that promised success, in order to maintain the economic importance of Germany as a production location. Today, BMW is leading in the individual mobility sector. The central message is transported via the brand slogan: "sheer driving pleasure". This assertion implies the most desirable and most important challenge, to develop technically and aesthetically convincing automobiles and to offer the customer a performance that reaches far beyond the joy of driving. It is the overcoming of the apparent contradiction

Von der Design-Skizze zum Prototyp: BMW Ingenieure und Designer arbeiten in der Entwicklung nicht nur mit virtuellen 3D-Animationen. Dreidimensionale Clay-Modelle sind für die optische und haptische Wahrnehmung maßgeblich.

und den Kunden eine Leistung anzubieten, die weit über die Fahrfreude hinaus geht. Es ist die Überwindung des scheinbaren Widerspruchs zwischen Vernunft und Leidenschaft, Verantwortung und Lebensgenuss, die BMW so einzigartig macht. Die Kraft des Unternehmens liegt auch im respektvollen Umgang mit seinen Produkten und Kunden. Wertschätzung und Individualität, Verlangen nach Schönheit und technische Perfektion, der Blick für kleinste Details – das sind die Gründe, warum die Marke überzeugt und Freude auslöst. Freude vermittelt auch die BMW Welt, in der Fahrzeuge und Markenthemen, Architektur und sinnliches Erleben eine perfekte Verbindung eingehen. Sie steht für alles, was BMW ausmacht und führt die spannende Geschichte der Marke fort. Zur Premiere der BMW 7er-Reihe erschien 1986 ein Buch über die Entwicklungsgeschichte dieser großen Limousine. Der Titel lautet „Die sieben Jahre des 7ers". Denn sieben Jahre hatte es gedauert, um die Quintessenz aus Größe und Eleganz, Leistung und Agilität zu bilden. Heute realisiert BMW diese Prozesse bei stetig komplexer werdenden Anforderungen an innovative Lösungen sowie an das Design und die Qualität der Produkte in der Hälfte der Zeit. Denn im internationalen Wettbewerb um Marktanteile zählt nicht nur das Gesamtkonzept eines Automobils.

Über seinen Erfolg entscheidet auch die Zeit von der Entwicklung eines neuen Modells bis zur Markteinführung. Wer insbesondere im Premiumsegment neue Produkte schneller als andere entwickelt, testet und produziert, ist seinen Mitbewerbern einen entscheidenden Schritt voraus. Trotz kürzerer Entwicklungszeiten nimmt die Komplexität der Technik ständig zu. Innovative elektronische Assistenten sorgen für funktionellen Komfort und entspanntes Fahren und navigieren das Automobil sicher durch den Verkehr. Zukünftig wird jedoch auch die Kommunikation des Automobils mit anderen Fahrzeugen, mit der Verkehrsleitzentrale, mit dem eigenen Büro oder der Familie noch mehr an Bedeutung gewinnen. Der Zugang zum Internet im Fahrzeug ist bereits Alltag, die Internetnavigation per Spracherkennung schon lange keine Theorie mehr. Mit den Möglichkeiten der Technik könnte auch die Anzahl der Knöpfe, Anzeigen und Schalter steigen. Aber die BMW Ingenieure haben bei aller technischen Raffinesse eines immer im Blick: die Freude am Fahren. Deshalb funktionieren die meisten Hightech-Aggregate nicht nur geräuschlos, sie arbeiten auch weitgehend unsichtbar. In der Regel genügen ein kleiner Bildschirm und wenige Handbewegungen mit einem einzigen Knopf, dem so genannten Controller, um einzustellen, was für den Fahrer wichtig ist. Diese effiziente Lösung ist das Ergebnis eines langen Entwicklungsprozesses. Er beginnt mit der Idee und einer genauen Leistungsbeschreibung, wird weitergeführt mit Designentwürfen und Computeranimationen. Funktionsmodelle werden konstruiert und Prototypen gebaut, bis endlich der Weg zum serienreifen Modell frei ist. Der Startschuss für solche Prozesse fällt während der Impulsphase. In diesem Stadium spüren BMW Scouts an Universitäten und Forschungsinstituten auf der ganzen Welt Trends auf und identifizieren dabei neue Technologien. Jede Idee wird dann von Spezialisten auf ihre automobile Tauglichkeit geprüft, bewertet und im besten Fall bis zur Serienreife weiterentwickelt. Dank globaler Vernetzung und modernster technischer Unterstützung benötigt diese Entwicklung inzwischen nur noch 30 Monate hochkonzentrierter Arbeit. Was BMW dabei leistet, zeigt ein Gang durch das Forschungs- und Innovationszentrum im

*From draft design to prototype: BMW engineers and designers work in the
development phase not only with virtual 3D animations. Three-dimensional
clay models are decisive for optical and haptic perspicacity.*

between reason and passion, responsibility and enjoyment of life that BMW so uniquely achieves. The company's
energy also comes from its respectful interaction with its products and customers. Esteem and individuality, the
desire for technical perfection and beauty, an eye for the smallest details – these are the reasons why the brand
is convincing and arouses delight. The BMW Welt also imparts delight, where vehicles and brand themes, architecture and sensual experience combine in perfect harmony. It stands for all that which BMW represents and
carries the exciting story of the brand onward. For the premiere of the BMW 7 Series a book was published in
1986 about the development history of this great limousine. Its title is "The Seven Years of the 7 Series", since
it had taken seven years to craft such a quintessence of grandeur and elegance, performance and agility. Today,
BMW implements these processes in only half the time, despite continually more complex demands on innovative solutions as well as on the design and the quality of the products. Indeed, in the international competition
for market shares, it is not only the overall concept of an automobile that counts.

Decisive upon its success is also the length of time from development of a new model to its introduction onto the market. Particularly in the premium segment, whoever develops, tests and produces faster than
the others remains a decisive step ahead of the competition. Despite shorter development times, the complex-
ity of the technology is continually increasing. Innovative electronic aids ensure functional comfort and relaxed
driving, and they navigate the automobile safely through the traffic. In future however, communication of the
automobile with other vehicles, with the traffic control centre or with one's own office or family will gain more
significance. Vehicle Internet access is already routine, Internet navigation via speech recognition has been
more than just a theory for some time now. With increasing technical possibilities, the number of buttons, displays and switches could also increase. However, with all their technical sophistication, BMW engineers always
have one thing in focus: driving pleasure. This is why most high-tech components operate not only silently, they
also generally function unseen. As a rule, a small screen and a few manual adjustments of a single knob, the
so-called controller, suffice to arrange those settings which are important to the driver. The result of a long
development process is so convincingly simple. It begins with the idea and an exact description of its performance, it is further elaborated with design concepts and computer animations. Functional models are constructed
and prototypes are built, until finally the way ahead is clear and the model is ready to go into production. The
starting signal for such processes occurs during the impulse phase. At this stage, BMW scouts at universities
and research institutes around the world track down trends, and in so doing identify new technologies. All ideas
are then tested by specialists for their automotive suitability, evaluated and at best further developed until they
are ready to go into production. Thanks to global networking and cutting-edge technical support, these develop-
ments meanwhile require as little as 30 months of highly concentrated effort. What BMW thereby achieves is
revealed by a visit to its Forschungs- und Innovationszentrum (Research and Innovation Centre, also known by
its German abbreviation FIZ) in North Munich. The technological heart of the BMW Group beats here on this
research campus, one of the world's most modern automobile-industry development centres. The building,

Münchner Norden. Das 1980 von Prof. Dr. Gunter Henn gemeinsam mit BMW Ingenieuren entworfene Gebäude ist eine Zukunftswerkstatt mit dem Ausmaß einer kleinen Technischen Universität. Mehr als 10.000 Menschen entwickeln dort aus innovativen Technologien Automobile, Motorräder und Verkehrskonzepte von morgen. 1986 wurde im ersten Bauabschnitt des Forschungs- und Innovationszentrum (FIZ) die Arbeit aufgenommen. Oktagonale Gebäude für Designstudios und Konstruktionsbüros umschließen einen Trakt für Werkstätten und Labore. Beide Bereiche sind durch Brücken verbunden. So findet das Planen, Entwerfen, Konstruieren und Testen nur wenige Schritte voneinander entfernt statt, wodurch Effizienz und Effektivität der zusammenhängenden Prozesse entscheidend erhöht werden. Das FIZ wird ständig optimiert und erweitert, um die Herausforderungen der Zukunft auch weiterhin erfolgreich annehmen zu können. Erst vor wenigen Jahren entstand das zentrale Entwicklungsgebäude, das so genannte Projekthaus. Hier bündelt BMW nicht nur sein Know-how für Fahrzeugtechnologien. Auch die Arbeitsbedingungen werden stetig verbessert, um neue Ideen für Produkte und Systeme in die Praxis umzusetzen. Etwa zur gleichen Zeit nahm das Prüfstandsgebäude seine Arbeit auf, das über einen riesigen Windkanal und ein neues Kompetenzzentrum für Motoren verfügt.

Der „Think Tank" des BMW Forschungs- und Entwicklungsverbundes wird von einem weltumspannenden Netzwerk aus spezialisierten Außenstellen unterstützt, die eng mit universitären und staatlichen Forschungseinrichtungen zusammenarbeiten. Direkt neben dem Forschungs- und Innovationszentrum entwickeln BMW Spezialisten gemeinsam mit Entwicklungspartnern Software-Lösungen für neue Elektronik-Konzepte. Mit dem Bau dieses Zentrums für Informationstechnologie (Car IT) bündelt BMW ab 2009 im Münchner Norden die IT-Aktivitäten für mehr als 3.000 Beschäftigte. Nur wenige Kilometer entfernt steuert die BMW Forschung und Technik GmbH die Forschungsthemen der BMW Group. Rund 250 Spezialisten haben hier einen klaren Auftrag: Sie entwickeln neue Technologien für die automobile Zukunft. Zu den Schlüsselthemen gehören Intelligentes Energiemanagement und Alternative Antriebe (BMW EfficientDynamics), Wasserstofftechnologie (BMW CleanEnergy) sowie Fahrerassistenzsysteme und Aktive Sicherheit (BMW ConnectedDrive). Das Institut für Mobilitätsforschung Berlin ist dagegen eine Einrichtung der BMW Group, die sich ausschließlich mit den künftigen Entwicklungen auf dem Gebiet der Mobilität beschäftigt. Dabei stellt Auto-Mobilität nur eine Facette von vielen dar. Sozial-, kultur- und gesellschaftspolitische Fragestellungen werden hier ebenfalls bearbeitet. Auf den Gebieten der Informations- und Telekommunikationstechnologie hat sich BMW im südfranzösischen Technologiepark Sophia Antipolis mit dem intereuropäischen Institut Eurecom zusammengeschlossen. Damit stärkt das Unternehmen sein Know-how innerhalb der Fahrzeug-IT, Telekommunikation und Mikroelektronik und dehnt sein Kooperationsfeld mit Hochschulen, Forschungsinstituten und Industrieunternehmen in Europa weiter aus. Im kalifornischen Palo Alto unterhält das Unternehmen ein Technology Office. Hier werden Themen wie Mechatronik, „Human Machine Interfaces" und Fahrerassistenzsysteme erarbeitet. Aus Oxnard im Silicon Valley liefert das „Engineering and Emission Test Center" neueste Erkenntnisse zur Schadstoffverringerung. Nicht weit davon entfernt feilt BMW Group Designworks, Newbury Park, USA an neuen Designstudien. Ein weiteres Büro für gestalterische Trends

An international innovation network: The BMW Research and Development System is assisted by specialists from all around the world. The Research and Innovation Centre (FIZ) in Munich works closely together with the Technology Office, Palo Alto and BMW Group Designworks, Newbury Park, USA.

designed in 1980 by Prof. Dr. Gunter Henn together with BMW engineers, is a workshop of the future with the dimensions of a small technical university. Here, using innovative technologies, more than 10,000 people are developing tomorrow's automobiles, motorbikes and traffic concepts. In 1986, work on the first construction phase of FIZ was begun. Octagonal buildings for design studios and construction offices surround a tract of workshops and laboratories. Both areas are interconnected by bridges, and planning, conception, construction and testing thus take place only a few paces away from each other, whereby efficiency and effectiveness of inter-connecting processes are decisively increased. The Research and Innovation Centre is constantly optimised and expanded in order to further enable challenges of the future to be successfully taken up. The central develop-ment building, the so-called Projekthaus (project house) came into being only a few years ago and is now being integrated into existing processes and functions as a new focal point. It is not only BMW's competence for vehi-cle technology that is integrated here: working conditions as well are continually improved in order to put new ideas for products and systems into practice. At approximately the same time, the test bed building – with an enormous wind tunnel and a new centre of excellence for engines at its disposal – began its operations.

The 'think tank' of the BMW Research and Development System is supported by a globally reaching net-work of specialised branches that cooperate closely with state and university research establishments. Directly beside the Research and Innovation Centre, BMW specialists together with development partners are developing software solutions for new electronic concepts. With the construction of this Zentrum für Informationstechnolo-gie (Centre for Information Technology, the so-called BMW Car IT), from 2009 BMW will be concentrating its IT-activities in North Munich for more than 3,000 employees. Only a few miles away, BMW Forschung und Technik GmbH (BMW Group Research and Technology) manages the research topics of the BMW Group. Here, around 250 specialists have a clear remit: They develop new technologies for the automotive future. Intelligent energy management and alternative powertrains (BMW EfficientDynamics), hydrogen technologies (BMW CleanEnergy) as well as driver assistance systems and active safety (BMW ConnectedDrive) are all core topics. The Institute for Mobility Research in Berlin is in contrast an establishment of the BMW Group that devotes itself to future develop-ments in the mobility sector. At the same time, automobility represents only one of many facets. Social, cultural and sociopolitical questions are likewise processed here. In the areas of information- and telecommunication technology, BMW has consolidated itself with the Inter-European Institute Eurecom in the Sophia Antipolis tech-nology park in Southern France. Thus, the company strengthens its know-how within the vehicle-IT sector, tele-communications and micro-electronics, and further extends its sphere of cooperation with universities, research institutes and industrial enterprises in Europe. In Palo Alto, California, the company maintains a technology office. Topics such as mechatronics, "human machine interfaces" and driver assistance systems are investi-gated here. The primary assignment of the "Engineering and Emission Test Center" in Oxnard, Silicon Valley, is the functional and continuous testing of vehicles and components, and it provides the latest findings on emis-sion reduction. Not much further away, the BMW Group Designworks in Newbury Park, USA, is improving upon

Effiziente Technologien: Mit einer umweltschonenden Energiestrategie setzt das Unternehmen auf technische Innovationen für mehr Freude am Fahren bei geringerem Verbrauch und verminderten Emissionen.

wird in Tokio unterhalten. BMW EfficientDynamics ist seit Jahren einer der wichtigsten Innovationsschwerpunkte des Unternehmens. Voraussetzungen für die Symbiose aus gesteigerter Fahrfreude und höherer Wirtschaftlichkeit sind eine neue Generation hocheffizienter Motoren, eine noch bessere Aerodynamik, ein innovativer Leichtbau und ein intelligentes Energiemanagement im Fahrzeug. Mit einer neuen Benzin-Einspritztechnologie sowie der Auto Start Stop Funktion, mit der Rückgewinnung von Bremsenergie und der Schaltpunktanzeige gelang es BMW, den Ausstoß von Kohlenstoffdioxid deutlich zu senken. Zur Eröffnung der BMW Welt umfasste die Produktpalette des Unternehmens bereits 22 Modelle mit einem Ausstoß von weniger als 140 g Kohlenstoffdioxid pro Kilometer. Mit diesen Aktivitäten unterstützt BMW die Kyoto-Ziele und arbeitet intensiv an der Senkung des Flottenverbrauches. Das ist aber nur die erste Stufe der Energiestrategie des Konzerns. Mittelfristig realisiert das Unternehmen zusätzliche Verbrauchsvorteile durch die weitere Elektrifizierung des Antriebsstrangs bis hin zur Hybridisierung, also dem intelligenten Management von Energieströmen im Fahrzeug. Mit dem BMW Concept X6 ActiveHybrid werden der Verbrennungsmotor und zwei leistungsstarke Elektromotoren erstmals so miteinander kombiniert, dass der Effizienzvorteil der Hybridtechnik innerhalb eines deutlich größeren Geschwindigkeitsbereiches genutzt werden kann als bei herkömmlichen Hybrid-Fahrzeugen. Langfristig strebt die BMW Group die Nutzung von Wasserstoff als Kraftstoff der Zukunft an. Bereits Ende der 1970er Jahre entwickelte BMW umweltschonende Automobile mit Wasserstoff-Verbrennungsmotor. 30 Jahre später erreicht die Umorientierung vom Erdöl zu einer klimaneutralen Energie-Technologie einen weiteren Höhepunkt. Mit dem BMW Hydrogen 7 präsentierte BMW im November 2006 die erste mit Wasserstoff angetriebene und damit praktisch emissionsfrei nutzbare Luxuslimousine für den Straßenverkehr. Dieses Automobil verfügt über einen Wasserstoff-Verbrennungsmotor, der sowohl mit Wasserstoff als auch mit Benzin betrieben werden kann.

Vom Rohblech bis zum fertigen Automobil sind viele komplexe Arbeitsschritte notwendig. Optimierte Fertigungsprozesse und Hightech in den Montagehallen machen aus jedem Fahrzeug ein Einzelstück. Hat der Kunde sich bei seinem Händler für die Ausstattung entschieden, bestätigt das Order-System das Produktionsdatum. Trotzdem sind Änderungswünsche zur Karosserievariante, zum Motor, zur Farbe oder Ausstattung noch bis sechs Tage vor Montagestart möglich. BMW Kunden nutzen diese Flexibilität sehr intensiv. In den Produktionsstätten entstehen unter Einhaltung kompromissloser Qualitätsrichtlinien Automobile mit individuellem Charakter. Höchstens zwei Fahrzeuge pro Jahr sind identisch. Dank dieser logistischen Meisterleistung erhält jeder Kunde zum Wunschtermin sein individuell auf ihn zugeschnittenes BMW Automobil. Die BMW Automobile der 7er, 6er und 5er Reihen werden in Dingolfing, Niederbayern, produziert. Im BMW Stammwerk in München laufen an jedem Arbeitstag mehr als 900 Fahrzeuge der 3er-Reihe vom Band. Dabei wird der 3er BMW ebenso wie die BMW 1er-Reihe auch in den Werken Regensburg und Leipzig sowie in Rosslyn, Südafrika, gefertigt. Der BMW X3 und der BMW X5 kommen aus dem amerikanischen Werk Spartanburg in South Carolina. Der Vorteil dieser lokalen Fertigung liegt in der Chance, neue Märkte mit langfristigem Wachstumspotenzial zu erschließen. BMW verfolgt diese Strategie auf der ganzen Welt und unterhält Montagewerke in Russland, Ägypten, Indien,

Efficient technologies: With an environmentally friendly energy strategy, the company relies on technical innovations for even more driving pleasure with less wastage and reduced emissions.

new design studies. A further office for creative trends is maintained in Tokyo. For some years now, BMW EfficientDynamics has been one of the company's most important focal points for innovation. The requirements for the symbiosis of increased driving pleasure and higher cost effectiveness are a new generation of highly efficient engines, even better aerodynamics, an innovative lightweight design and an intelligent energy management within the vehicle. With a new gasoline injection technology as well as the Auto Start Stop function, and with the recovery of braking energy and the gearshift indicator, BMW was able to significantly reduce carbon dioxide emissions. When the BMW Welt was opened, the company's product range already included 22 models with an emission level of less than 140g carbon dioxide per kilometre. With such activities BMW supports the Kyoto targets and works intensively on the reduction of its average fleet consumption. This is however only the first step in the company's energy strategy. In the medium term BMW implements additional consumption benefits via further electrification of the powertrain right up to hybridisation, thus the intelligent management of energy currents within the vehicle. In the BMW Concept X6 ActiveHybrid, the combustion engine and two high-performance electromotors are combined for the first time in such a way that the efficiency benefits of hybrid technology can be used within a significantly larger speed range than in conventional hybrid vehicles. In the long term, the BMW Group seeks to utilise hydrogen as the fuel of the future. BMW had already developed environmentally friendly automobiles with hydrogen combustion engines towards the end of the 1970s. 30 years later, the reorientation from petroleum to a climate-neutral energy technology reached a further peak: With the BMW Hydrogen 7, the company presented in November 2006 the first hydrogen-powered luxury limousine, thereby practically emission-free for road use. This automobile has a hydrogen combustion engine that can be fuelled by hydrogen as well as by gasoline.

From sheet metal to complete automobile: many complex individual operations are necessary. Optimised manufacturing processes and high-tech in the assembly halls produce individual vehicles in each case. When the customer has decided upon the desired optional-component version with his dealer, the order system will confirm the production date. Nevertheless, desired changes to bodywork variants, motor, colour and equipment are possible up to six days before the beginning of assembly. BMW customers make thorough use of this flexibility. Automobiles with individual character emerge in the production facilities via strict compliance to quality guidelines. Two vehicles per year at the most are identical. Thanks to this logistic feat, on the desired day each customer receives an individual and personally tailored BMW automobile. The BMW automobiles of the 7, 6 and 5 Series are produced in Dingolfing, Lower Bavaria. In the BMW home plant in Munich, more than 900 vehicles of the 3 Series roll off the assembly line each day. The 3 Series, as well as the BMW 1 Series, is also assembled in the plants at Regensburg and Leipzig as well as in Rosslyn, South Africa. The BMW X3 and the BMW X5 come from the US plant in Spartanburg, South Carolina. The advantage of this local production is the chance to break into new markets with long-term growth potential. BMW follows this strategy all around the world and maintains assembly plants in Russia, Egypt, India, Thailand, Malaysia and China. Altogether, more than a million BMW

*Chronologie der Einzigartigkeit: Aus tonnenschweren Stahlrollen,
so genannten Coils, werden Automobilteile gefertigt, zu einer Karosserie
zusammengefügt und lackiert. Erst nach zahlreichen Qualitäts-
tests wird das Automobil mit dem Markenzeichen ausgestattet.*

Thailand, Malaysia und in China. Insgesamt entstehen jährlich über eine Million BMW Automobile an zwei Dut-
zend Standorten in 13 Ländern. Diese Werke beliefern Vertriebsgesellschaften und BMW Importeure in 120
Ländern. Dabei produziert kein BMW Werk alle zur Fertigung eines neuen Automobils erforderlichen Teile
selbst. Die Fertigungsstätten arbeiten in einem Produktionsnetzwerk zusammen und werden außerdem von
Zulieferern unterstützt. Auf vier Kontinenten sind jeden Tag Lastwagen, Güterzüge und Flugzeuge für BMW
unterwegs, um Einzelteile untereinander auszutauschen und die BMW Werke mit zusätzlich benötigten Kompo-
nenten zu versorgen.

Chronology of inimitability: Automobile parts are manufactured from heavy coils of sheet steel, which are then assembled into a car's bodywork and painted. Only after numerous quality tests is the vehicle provided with the brand's trademark.

automobiles are produced annually at two dozen locations in 13 countries. These plants supply marketing companies and BMW importers in 120 countries. At the same time, no single BMW plant itself produces all the parts necessary for assembly of a new automobile. The assembly plants work together in a production network and are furthermore supported by suppliers. Every day on four continents, trucks, freight trains and aircraft are in transit for BMW, in order to exchange individual parts amongst each other and to supply the BMW plants with additionally required components.

eine vision wird wirklichkeit. die BMW Welt _ a vision comes true. the BMW Welt

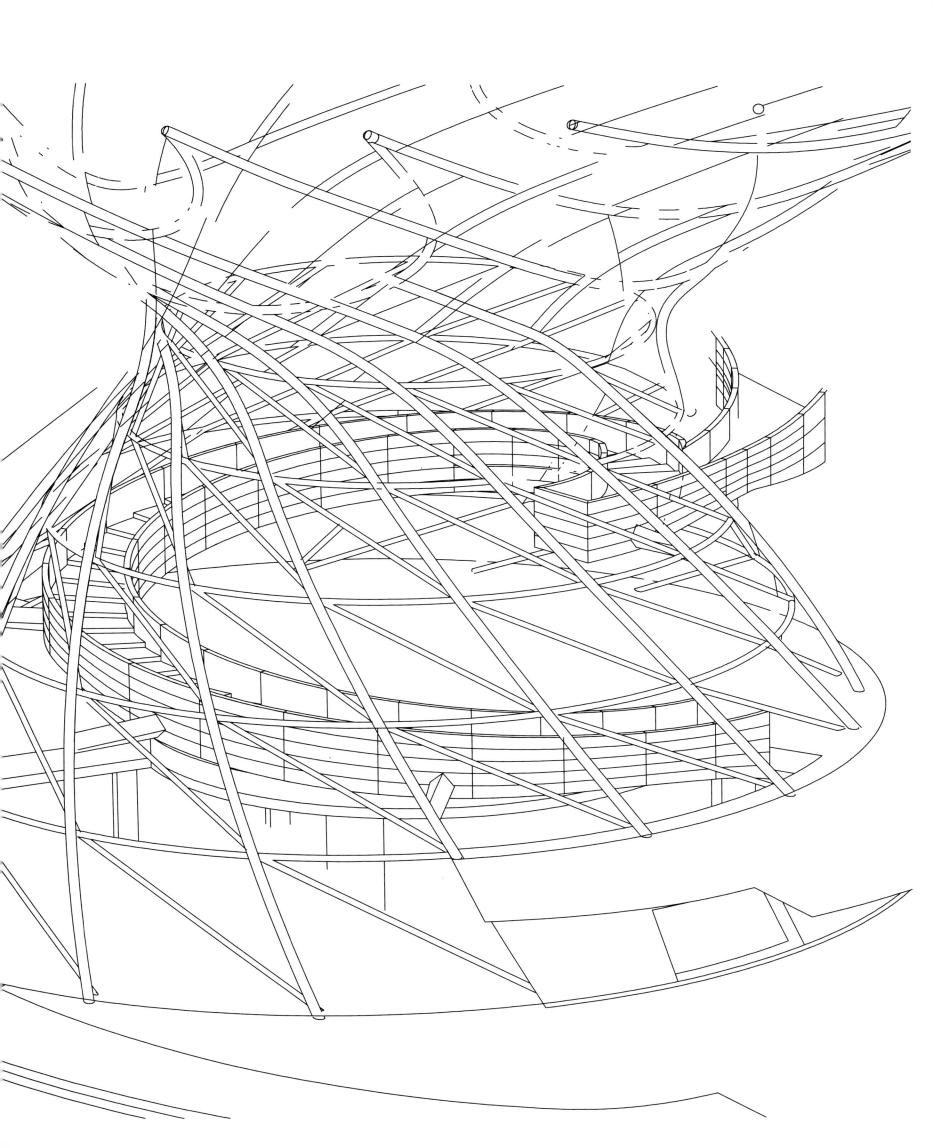

räume für träume _ space for dreams

räume für träume _ space for dreams

Bei der Entstehung der BMW Welt war der besondere Pulsschlag von BMW von Anfang an spürbar. Das außergewöhnliche Format des Projektes war das Ergebnis der hohen Ansprüche des Unternehmens. Heute ist die Erlebnisdimension des Bauwerks ein Höhepunkt der automobilen Kultur und das zukunftsweisende Gebäude gibt der modernen Architektur die Richtung vor. Bereits die Planung und Realisierung haben große Emotionen und ein eindrucksvolles Echo in der Öffentlichkeit hervorgerufen.

When the BMW Welt emerged, BMW's vibrant pulse was noticeable from the very beginning. The extraordinary size of the project was the result of the high aspirations of the company. Today, the experience aspect of the building is a highlight of automobile culture, and the future-oriented building sets the course in modern architecture. Even the planning and realization have aroused strong emotions and an impressive echo in the public sphere.

Sauerbruch Hutton Architekten, Berlin, 1. Preis: Die drei Brennpunkte „event", „exhibition" und „performance" sind unter einem weit ausgreifenden Dach zusammengefasst. Darunter befinden sich drei unterschiedlich amorph geformte Glaszylinder.

Mit der Entscheidung des Unternehmens für den Bau der BMW Welt Ende der 1990er Jahre rückte ein Aspekt sehr schnell in den Mittelpunkt der Gespräche: Die Frage des perfekten Standortes. Das Erlebnis BMW braucht kein Projekt auf der „grünen Wiese", irgendwo draußen vor der Stadt. Das Oberwiesenfeld in Milbertshofen ist der Ort, an dem der Puls von BMW seit über 90 Jahren schlägt. Hier standen 1917 die ersten Werkhallen des Unternehmens. Die Geschichte der Marke hat auf diesem Gelände nicht nur ihren Anfang genommen. Von der Konzernzentrale wird seit mehr als 30 Jahren auch nachhaltig die Zukunft gestaltet. Nur in unmittelbarer Nachbarschaft von Vierzylinder, Stammwerk und Museum konnte das Erlebnis- und Auslieferungszentrum entstehen. Denn hier ist die Marke zu Hause. Der Standort der BMW Welt liegt an einer der Verkehrshauptschlagadern Münchens, dem Mittleren Ring. Direkt dahinter erstreckt sich das Münchner BMW Werk, das täglich von Lastwagen frequentiert wird und dadurch zum Verkehrsaufkommen beiträgt. Auch Busbahnhof und U-BahnStation sowie das dicht bewohnte Olympische Dorf beanspruchen die Verkehrswege in der Umgebung. Dass diese exponierte Lage noch eine weitere Belastung durch ein Erlebnis- und Auslieferungszentrum verträgt, wurde von den verantwortlichen Stellen der Stadt München deshalb zunächst bezweifelt. Denn ein Gebäude, das pro Jahr mehr als 800.000 Gäste anzieht, wird zwangsläufig zusätzlichen Verkehr erzeugen. Dabei sind hier die jährlich 45.000 fabrikneuen Automobile noch nicht berücksichtigt, die auf Tiefladern erst angeliefert werden müssen, bevor ihre neuen Besitzer mit ihnen die BMW Welt verlassen.

Die Bedenken der Stadt galten nicht den Automobilen der Gäste, die das Verkehrssystem an dieser Stelle zusätzlich nutzen. Bei 130.000 Fahrzeugen, die jeden Tag über den Mittleren Ring fahren, waren aus Sicht der Verkehrsplaner 300 Automobile mehr zu verkraften. Der Lastwagenverkehr schien zunächst das Problem zu sein. Dafür entwickelte BMW eine pragmatische Lösung. Jeder Lastwagen, der neue Automobile in der BMW Welt anliefert, verlässt das Gebäude direkt gegenüber der Einfahrt zum BMW Stammwerk. Die Lastwagen fahren also nicht zurück auf die Straße, sondern überqueren sie nur, um im Werk wieder mit neuen Fahrzeugen oder Fahrzeugteilen beladen zu werden. Damit war der verkehrstechnisch größte Einwand gegen die BMW Welt an dieser Stelle entkräftet, und die Vision des Unternehmens für das neue Erlebnis- und Auslieferungszentrum konnte langsam Gestalt annehmen. Premium-Architektur für eine Premium-Marke, das war der Anspruch des Architekturwettbewerbs, der 2001 von BMW zur Realisierung der BMW Welt ausgeschrieben wurde. Ziel war es, ein Bauwerk von herausragender Gestaltung und Organisation hervorzubringen, das gleichzeitig die Welt von BMW repräsentiert. Bevor das Ergebnis des Wettbewerbs tatsächlich umgesetzt werden konnte, präsentierte die Stadt das Projekt einer Kommission aus Architekten, die über die Stadtgestalt wacht. Diese Stadtgestaltungskommission kann Bauvorhaben beschleunigen, bei Einwänden aber auch erheblich verzögern. Fällt ein Entwurf durch, ist mit einer Baugenehmigung kaum zu rechnen. Ohne die Zustimmung der Kommission war an ein Vorhaben dieser Größe an der städtebaulich sensiblen Position gegenüber dem Münchner Olympiapark nicht zu denken. Daran ließ Münchens Oberbürgermeister Christian Ude keinen Zweifel. Gleichzeitig sagte er jedoch auch: „Wir wünschen uns dieses Projekt. Wir freuen uns, wenn es kommt. Wir werden das Wettbewerbsergebnis

With the company's decision at the end of the 1990s to build the BMW Welt, one aspect very quickly arose as a focal point in the talks: The question of the perfect location. The BMW experience does not require a greenfield development somewhere out of town. The Oberwiesenfeld in Munich's Milbertshofen district is the place at which BMW's heart has been beating for over 90 years. In 1917 the company's first factory buildings stood here. The history of the BMW brand had not only its beginnings on these grounds: From the headquarters, the future has been lastingly moulded here for more than 30 years. Only within the immediate vicinity of the BMW four-cylinder, home plant and museum was it possible for the event and delivery centre to emerge, since it is here that the BMW brand is at home. The location of the BMW Welt is situated at one of Munich's main traffic arteries, the Mittlerer Ring. The Munich BMW production plant spreads out directly behind it and is frequented daily by truck deliveries, which thereby add to the city's traffic volume. The nearby bus and underground stations as well as the high residential density of the Olympic village also make considerable use of transport routes within the surrounding area. That this prominent location could endure still one further burden from an event and delivery centre, it was therefore initially doubted by the department responsible for such matters in Munich. Indeed, a building that annually attracts more than 800,000 visitors would inevitably create additional traffic. This is not yet taking into account the 45,000 brand new automobiles each year, which must firstly be delivered by car-trans-porters, before their new owners drive off in them from the BMW Welt.

The city's concerns weren't about the visitors' cars that would additionally burden the traffic system at this location. With 130,000 automobiles using the Mittlerer Ring daily, an additional 300 automobiles, according to the traffic planners, could easily be dealt with. Initially, it was the truck traffic that appeared to be the problem, and BMW developed a pragmatic solution for it: Each truck that delivers new automobiles to the BMW Welt, exits the building directly opposite the entrance to the BMW home plant. The trucks therefore do not return along the street but simply cross over it, in order to be reloaded with new automobiles or car-parts in the plant. The greatest traffic-related objection to the BMW Welt was thereby invalidated at this point, and the company's vision for the new event and delivery centre could gradually begin to take shape. Premium architecture for a pre-mium brand of automobile – this was the requirement of the architectural competition that was announced in 2001 by BMW for the realisation of the BMW Welt. The aim was to create a building of outstanding design and organisation that at the same time would represent the world of BMW. Before the results of the competition could actually be realised, the city authorities presented the project to a commission of architects who keep watch over the cityscape. This city planning commission is able to speed up building developments, but can however severely delay those to which it has objections. If a design concept fails the commission's assessment, then building permission is barely to be expected. Without the commission's consent, a construction project of these dimensions at such a sensitive urban-planning location opposite Munich's Olympic Park, could not even begin to be contemplated. Munich's lord mayor, Christian Ude, made this point quite clear. At the same time he nevertheless also added: "We want this project. We will be very pleased if it goes ahead. We shall support the

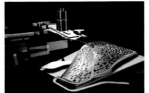

Zaha Hadid Ltd., London, 3. Preis: Der Gebäudekomplex vermittelt eine Mischung aus Inspiration und Gelassenheit – und will ein Moment der Verwunderung erzeugen. Das setzt die Bereitschaft voraus, sich auf ein neues räumliches Experiment einzulassen.

auf jede Art unterstützen." Wer einen so bedeutenden Wettbewerb ausschreibt, verspricht, sich an das Votum der Jury zu halten. Für BMW bedeutete das, eine Entscheidung von enormer Tragweite nicht mehr allein zu treffen. Das Unternehmen hatte schon für den Entwurf der Konzernzentrale Ende der 1960er Jahre einen Architekturwettbewerb ausgelobt. Eingeladen wurde jedoch nur eine Anzahl sorgfältig ausgewählter Architekten. Ausgerechnet die gewagte Hängekonstruktion von Prof. Dr. Karl Schwanzer überzeugte damals, und das eigentlich als Außenseiter angetretene Hängehaus schrieb Architekturgeschichte. Damit hatte niemand gerechnet. Doch Mut zahlt sich eben aus und das Unternehmen entschloss sich deshalb, für den Bau der BMW Welt ein noch größeres Risiko einzugehen. Der „Realisierungswettbewerb BMW Erlebnis- und Auslieferungszentrum" sollte diesmal uneingeschränkt zugänglich und international ausgerichtet sein. „Schaffen Sie ein Gebäude, das sich in respektvoller Harmonie in den Kontext der charakteristischen Architektur des Olympiaparks und der BMW Group einfügen lässt", hieß es in der Einladung an Architekten aus aller Welt. „Entwerfen Sie einen Komplex, der den dynamischen Charakter ebenso unverwechselbar ausdrückt wie das, was diese Marke zu vermitteln verspricht: Freude am Fahren." Diesem ebenso komplexen wie ungewöhnlichen Aufruf kamen 275 der weltbesten Architekten nach und reichten ihre Entwürfe ein. Nur jeder zehnte Vorschlag wurde von der Expertenjury für das weitere Auswahlverfahren zugelassen. Zu ihnen gehörte der Entwurf der in London arbeitenden Zaha Hadid, die kurze Zeit später für das Zentralgebäude des BMW Werkes in Leipzig verantwortlich zeichnete.

Alle 28 Entwürfe der ersten Auswahlrunde kennzeichnete eine harmonische und schlüssige Formgebung. Das Architekturbüro Morphosis aus Santa Monica, Kalifornien, setzte mit einem 200 mal 120 Meter großen und 22 Meter hohen Baukörper auf die Idee des Fließenden und der Bewegung. Ähnliche Überlegungen stellte Feichtinger Architectes aus Paris an. Ihr Entwurf glich einer dynamischen Welle. Das Münchner Büro Auer+Weber bewarb sich mit einer organischen Raumhülle, die rund und weich wie ein Flusskiesel wirkt. Die Verbindung von der Konzernzentrale zum Olympiagelände verläuft hier laut Planung mitten durch das Gebäude. Die Architekten von MVRDV, Rotterdam, stellten einen Entwurf vor, der seinen dramaturgischen Höhepunkt an der himmelwärts strebenden Gebäudekante findet. Die Intention der Architekten war es, mit der Leichtigkeit dieser Bewegung die Dynamik des Windes zu symbolisieren. Der Entwurf des Berliner Büros Triad sah einen riesigen Bogen aus Beton und Glas vor, der den linsenförmigen Baukörper in seinem Zentrum umschließt. Sauerbruch Hutton Architekten präsentierte drei riesige Glaspavillons, die von einer gigantischen Dachkonstruktion zusammengefasst werden. Und aus Wien kam von Prof. Wolf D. Prix ein Vorschlag, mit dem der Architekt des Büros COOP HIMMELB(L)AU wieder einmal deutlich machte, warum es sich „die Rolling Stones der Architektur" nennt. Sein Vorschlag für das Gebäude war ebenso ausdrucksstark wie fantasievoll. Er zeigte über einem weitgehend verglasten Erdgeschoss eine riesige begehbare Wolke, die sich an ihrer prominentesten Stelle, gegenüber BMW Hochhaus und Museum, aus einem in sich gedrehten Doppelkegel aus Stahl und Glas heraus ergießt. Dieser Kegel schraubt sich aus dem Boden wie ein Wirbel, der die Besucher in das Gebäude hineinzusaugen scheint. Dieser Entwurf verließ die üblichen Gewohnheiten der Architektur so stark, dass erst einmal offen blieb, ob diese Idee überhaupt realisierbar

Zaha Hadid Ltd., London, 3rd prize: The building complex conveys a
blend of inspiration and serenity – and intends to create a moment of wonderment.
It implies the willingness to become involved in a new spatial experiment.

competition's conclusions in every way." Whoever announces such an important competition, promises to abide by the jury's decisions. This meant that for BMW, a decision of such momentousness would no longer be made alone. The company had already advertised an architectural competition for a design for its headquarters at the end of the 1960s. However, only a small number of carefully selected architects were invited to take part. Of all things, the bold suspended construction design by Prof. Dr. Karl Schwanzer proved to be the most convincing back then, and this suspended building, having practically only an outside chance at the time, wrote architectural history. No one had reckoned with such an outcome. However, boldness pays off and the company therefore decided to take an even greater risk in building the BMW Welt. This time, the BMW event and delivery centre architectural competition should not impose restrictions on the entrants and should be internationally oriented. "Create a building that integrates in deferential harmony into the context of the characteristic architecture of the Olympic Park and the BMW Group", it said in the invitation to architects all around the world. "Devise a complex which likewise unmistakeably expresses the dynamic character that the BMW brand itself pledges to convey: sheer driving pleasure." 275 of the world's best architects took up this equally complex as well as unusual challenge and submitted their concepts. Only one in ten of the drafts was accepted by the jury of experts for a further phase in the selection process. Among these was the draft concept by Zaha Hadid who, working in London, shortly thereafter became responsible for the central building of the BMW plant in Leipzig.

All 28 draft concepts from the first stage of selection indicated a harmonious and coherent design. The architectural bureau Morphosis in Santa Monica, California, with a building 200 by 120 metres in size and 22 metres high, relied on the idea of a flowing motion, and of movement. Feichtinger Architectes in Paris presented similar considerations. Their concept resembled a dynamic wave. The Munich architects Auer+Weber entered with an organic, spatial shell that appeared round and soft like a pebble. According to these plans, the connecting link between the group's headquarters and the Olympic Park would run right through the middle of the building. The architects from MVRDV of Rotterdam introduced a concept whose dramaturgical climax can be seen in the skyward-pointing edge of the building. The architects' intention was to symbolize the dynamics of the wind with the lightness of this movement. The concept from the Berlin architects, Triad, envisaged a giant concrete and glass arch encompassing a lenticular building in its centre. Sauerbruch Hutton Architects presented three enormous glass pavilions, conjoined by a giant roof construction. And from Vienna came a proposal by Prof. Wolf D. Prix with which the architect from COOP HIMMELB(L)AU once again made clear why this bureau calls itself "the Rolling Stones of architecture". His proposal for the building was as expressive as it was imaginative. It displayed above a largely glazed ground floor, a gigantic walk-through 'cloud' which, at its most prominent point – opposite the BMW tower and museum – pours out of a double cone of steel and glass entwined in itself. The cone screws itself out of the ground like a vortex that appears to suck the visitors into the building. This design concept departed from usual architectural practices so much that at first it remained unclear if the idea could be realised at all. In the competition's final stage of selection, the best eight concepts were further evaluated,

Morphosis, Santa Monica, 4. Preis: Die Verwebung von städtischer Struktur und weichen, groß angelegten Gesten ruft Bilder des Fließenden und der Bewegung hervor. Die hochkomplexe Architektursprache vermittelt ein beeindruckendes Raumerlebnis.

sein würde. In der finalen Auswahlrunde des Wettbewerbs kamen die besten acht Entwürfe zur Bewertung. Die Architekten waren eingeladen, ihre Ideen weiter zu konkretisieren. Stundenlange Gespräche fanden statt, in denen BMW erklärte, was aus Unternehmenssicht wesentlich war und realisierbar erschien. Die Phase des Überarbeitens und Überdenkens brachte jedes einzelne Projekt der Wirklichkeit ein großes Stück näher. Dann stand die Entscheidung der Jury an. Nur für vier der letzten acht Teilnehmer war eine Platzierung vorgesehen. Um die Gefahr zu vermeiden, sich mit dem ersten Preis an einen für das Unternehmen letztlich doch nicht realisierbaren Entwurf zu binden, entschieden sich der BMW Vorstand unter der Leitung des damaligen Vorstandsvorsitzenden Prof. Dr. Joachim Milberg und die Mitglieder der Jury für zwei Erstplatzierungen. Der Vorstand konnte eine Stichwahl zwischen den beiden ersten Preisen treffen. Realisiert wurde schließlich der Entwurf, der sich visionär und richtungweisend mit den Ideen identifiziert, die BMW mit dem Bauvorhaben verbindet, und der auch aus betrieblicher Sicht funktioniert.

Und wie schon in der Vergangenheit bewies das Unternehmen auch bei der BMW Welt Mut zum architektonischen Risiko. Die beiden kühnsten Entwürfe und ihre visionären Architekten wurden mit einem ersten Preis geehrt: Sauerbruch Hutton Architekten für die gläsernen Hüllen und offenen Passagen unter einem weit ausladenden Dach und COOP HIMMELB(L)AU für die begehbare Wolke. Nun lag die Entscheidung bei BMW. Wollte man die kultivierte und mit Sicherheit umsetzbare Idee aus Berlin realisieren oder den spektakulären, avantgardistischeren Wiener Entwurf – auch auf die Gefahr hin, mit diesem Projekt Architektur und Baukunst neu zu definieren? Schon die Berechnung dieses an keiner Stelle senkrechten oder rechtwinkligen Gebäudes war eine Herausforderung für die moderne Computertechnik. Die Aussicht war jedoch bestechend: Eine Premium-Marke wie BMW wird in Szene gesetzt mit einer Architektur, die Grenzen sprengt. Die Verantwortlichen waren von der Fantasie, der Begeisterung, der Kühnheit und der visionären Kraft dieses Gebäudes bereits überzeugt. Die Wolke hatte gewonnen.

 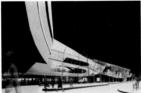 

Morphosis, Santa Monica, 4th prize:
The interweaving of urban structure and soft, large-scale
gestures evokes images of fluid movement and animation.
The highly complex architectural language imparts
an impressive spatial experience.

and their architects were invited to further substantiate their ideas. Talks took place which lasted hours, in which BMW explained what, in the company's view, was essential and what appeared to be feasible. The reworking and reconsideration phase brought each individual project considerably closer to reality. Then it was time for the jury to decide. Placement was provided for only four of the final eight participants. In order to avoid the danger of commitment to a first-prize concept, which would ultimately turn out to be unfeasible for the company, the BMW board of directors – under the leadership of chief executive Prof. Dr. Joachim Milberg and the members of the jury – decided to award two first-prizes. The board then carried out a run-off vote between the two first-prize entries. The concept that was ultimately implemented was the one which, in a visionary and trendsetting way, identified with the ideas BMW associates with the building project, and which would work well in operational terms.

And as in the past, the company demonstrated with the BMW Welt a boldness in the face of architectural risk. Both of these very audacious concepts and their visionary architects were honoured with a first prize: Sauerbruch Hutton for the glazed exterior surfaces and open passages under a spaciously projecting roof, and COOP HIMMELB(L)AU for the walk-through 'cloud'. Now BMW had to make the decision. Was it desirable to realise the cultivated and certainly feasible idea from Berlin or the spectacular, more avantgarde Viennese concept – even at the risk of redefining architecture and building construction with this project? Even the calculations for a building without any perpendiculars or right-angles were a challenge for modern computer technology. The prospects were however impressive: A premium brand such as BMW is superimposed onto an architectural scheme which breaks all the rules. Those responsible were already strongly convinced by the fantasy, enthusiasm, audacity and the visionary power of this building. The 'cloud' had won through.

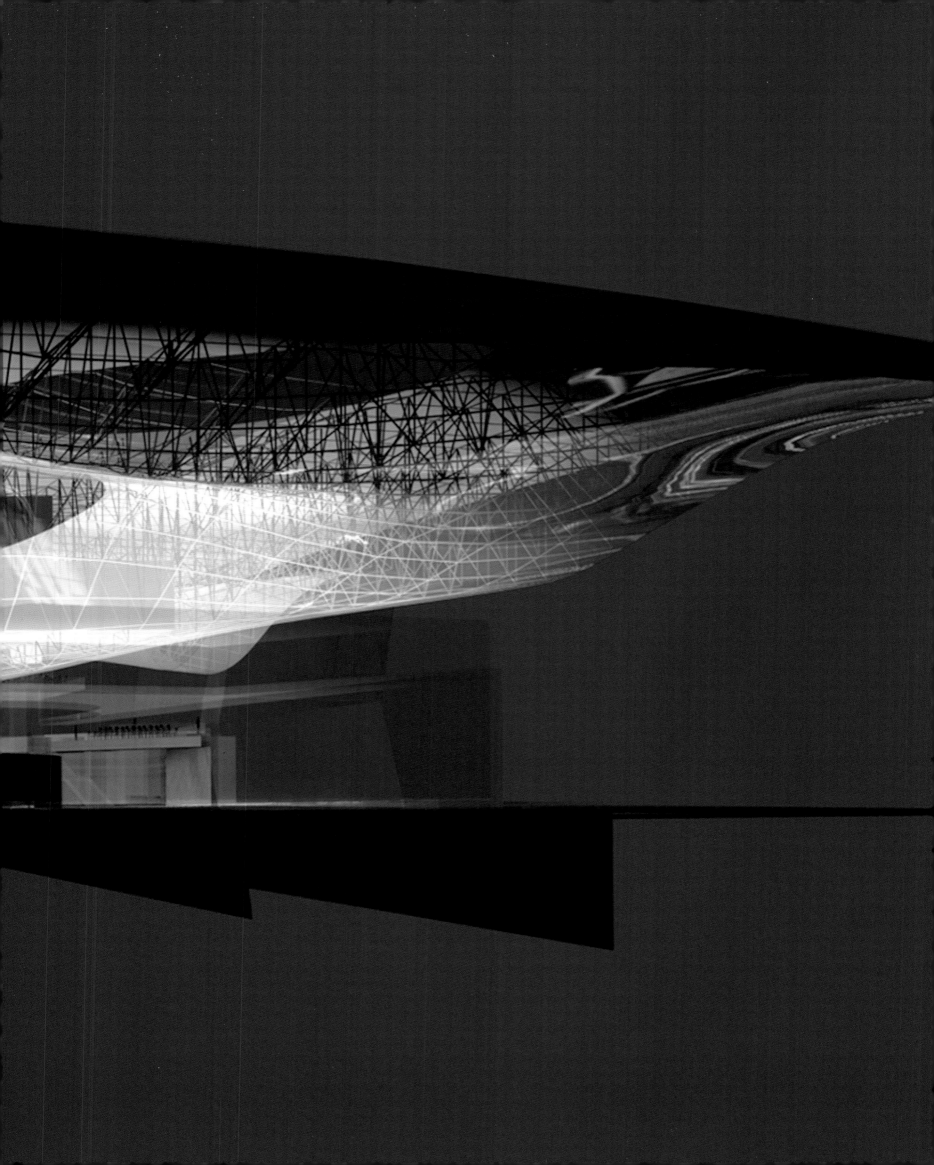

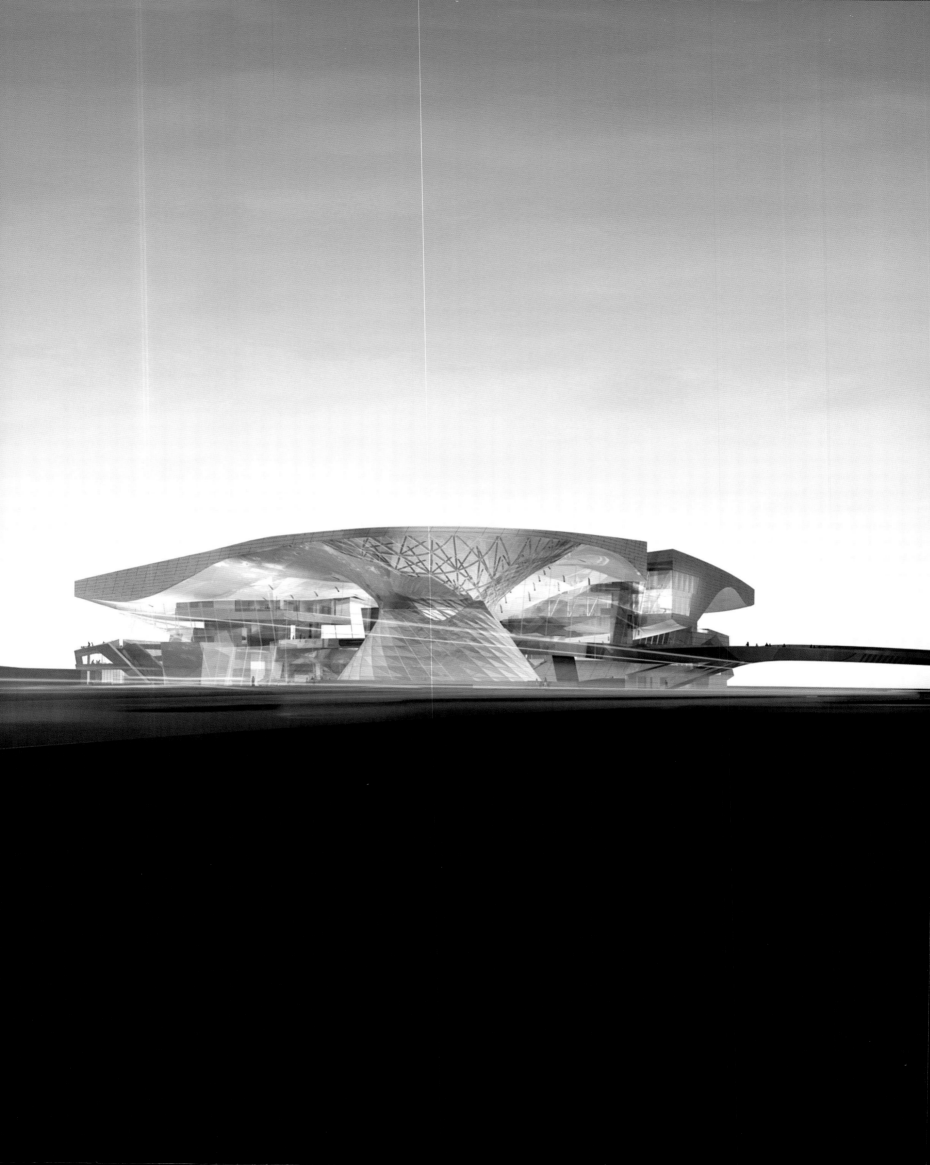

➤ 56/57 *Unwirklich und voller Energie: Das Dachtragwerk (Computeranimation).*
Unreal and full of energy: The roof structure (computer animation).

➤ 58/59 *Architektur und Kunst: Das Modell der BMW Welt beeindruckte bereits in der Planungsphase im Herbst 2002 durch seine ungewöhnliche und zukunftsweisende Gestalt. Illuminiertes Modell, Ansicht Ost und Südost.*
Architecture and art: The model of the BMW Welt had already made an impression in the planning phase in autumn 2002 through its unusual and visionary design. Illuminated model, eastern and south-eastern perspective.

➤ 60/61 *Gefühlte Bewegung: Der zentrale Begriff für das Gebäude heißt Dynamik (Computeranimation).*
Perceived movement: The central concept for the building is dynamics (computer animation).

➤ 62/63 *Illumination eines architektonischen Glanzpunktes: Die BMW Welt bei Nacht vor der Kulisse der Landeshauptstadt (Computeranimation).*
Illumination of an architectural highlight: The BMW Welt at night in the urban setting of the state's capital (computer animation).

➤ 64 *Von Sturmwirbeln inspiriert: Der markante Doppelkegel an der südöstlichen Spitze des Gebäudes (Computeranimation).*
Inspired by a storm cyclone: The striking Double Cone at the south-eastern point of the building (computer animation).

von der vision zur realität _ from vision to reality

Der Architekturentwurf von Prof. Wolf D. Prix und COOP HIMMELB(L)AU für die BMW Welt ist eine großartige Vision, ihre Realisierung eine enorme technische und logistische Herausforderung. COOP HIMMELB(L)AU erarbeitete ein filigranes Meisterwerk aus Stahl und Glas, hart an der Grenze des Machbaren, herausfordernd und dynamisch wie die Marke, für die es steht. Architektur und Kommunikation bilden in der BMW Welt einen harmonischen Gleichklang. Mit dem Doppelkegel als optischem Höhepunkt hat sich das Gebäude ein Zentrum der Kraft geschaffen.

The architectural concept by Prof. Wolf D. Prix and COOP HIMMELB(L)AU for the BMW Welt is a magnificent vision, its realisation is an enormous technical and logistic challenge. COOP HIMMELB(L)AU has produced an intricate, graceful masterpiece from steel and glass, pressing hard against the limits of the feasible. Challenging and dynamic, just like the brand that it represents. Architecture and communication stand together in the BMW Welt in a harmonious accord. With the Double Cone as an optical highlight, the building as a whole has created a centre of energy.

Ein frühes Modell der Wolkenlandschaft: Das scheinbar schwebende Dach der BMW Welt steht als Symbol für Leichtigkeit und Transparenz. Architektur, die nicht nur offene Räume, sondern auch offenes Denken zulässt.

Eine Wolke zu bauen, die auf mehreren Ebenen begehbar sein wird, ist eine große Aufgabe. Im Dezember 2001 fielen die letzten Entscheidungen für den Bau der BMW Welt. Einen Monat später begann die Realisierung. Aus Skizzen wurden Studien, aus Studien dreidimensionale Computergrafiken und aus virtuellen echte Architekturmodelle aus Hartholz und Plexiglas. Auf der Architektur-Biennale in Venedig 2002 wurde eines dieser Modelle erstmals der Öffentlichkeit präsentiert. Im Inneren des Gebäudes waren zwei winzige Videokameras installiert. Während sich das Modell langsam um sich selbst und um die Kameras drehte, wurden die Videobilder auf die umliegenden Wände projiziert. Sie zeigten Perspektiven aus der Innenwelt des Gebäudes und vermittelten dem Betrachter das Gefühl, bereits mitten in der BMW Welt zu stehen. In der Zwischenzeit wurde unermüdlich am Entwurf gefeilt. Die Architekten konstruierten das Zentrum des Gebäudes, die so genannte Plaza der BMW Welt. Die größte überdachte Bühne der Marke entstand. Unterhalb dieser riesigen Ausstellungs-, Erlebnis- und Auslieferungsfläche wurden aus zwei Untergeschossen zunächst drei, dann vier. Es galt eine zunehmende Anzahl von Funktionsräumen zu berücksichtigen. Die insgesamt 1.200 Türen des Gebäudes öffnen sich heute zu mehr als 1.000 Räumen. Der Großteil davon befindet sich unterhalb der Erdoberfläche, im Reich der Technik.

Im Zeichen der Technik stand auch das riesige Wolkendach der BMW Welt. Die ebene Konstruktion bot ideale Voraussetzungen für die Montage einer Fotovoltaikanlage, die eine Stromleistung von acht Megawatt erzeugt. Die Dachunterseite entwickelte sich im Inneren des Gebäudes einem Wellengebirge ähnlich mit Raumhöhen zwischen acht und zwanzig Metern. Wie ein umgedrehter Wolkenhügel senken sich Berge und Täler in das Gebäude hinein. Hier lässt sich an sonnigen Tagen das Funkeln des Lichtes beobachten, das sich in den achttausendfach verschweißten Stahlträgern bricht. Diese scheinbar schwebende Dachkonstruktion wiegt rund 4.000 Tonnen und wird dabei von nur elf filigranen Pfeilern getragen. Während die leistungsfähigsten Computer die Statik des Gebäudes berechneten, startete die Ausschreibung des Bauvorhabens. BMW vergab den Auftrag nicht an einen Generalunternehmer, sondern jedes Gewerk einzeln. Es wurden meterweise Verträge geschrieben. Im August 2003 rückten die ersten Bagger an und beseitigten zunächst das damalige Olympia Parkhaus, das sich auf dem Baugelände befand. Später waren hier Hunderte von Bauarbeitern gleichzeitig beschäftigt. Bohrpfähle wurden gesetzt, um die Ränder der so genannten „weißen Wanne" abzustützen, in die das Fundament der BMW Welt gegossen werden sollte. Kubikmeterweise wurde Erdreich entfernt und Lastwagen für Lastwagen abtransportiert. Im Mai 2004 war die Talsohle der Baugrube erreicht: 14 Meter tief und so groß wie vier Fußballfelder. Der Grundstein konnte gelegt werden. Am 16. Juli 2004 fand die Feierstunde statt, zu der die Honoratioren der Stadt München eingeladen waren. Der damalige bayerische Ministerpräsident Edmund Stoiber und Münchens Oberbürgermeister Christian Ude beglückwünschten BMW zum „architektonischen Highlight". Die BMW Welt, so der Oberbürgermeister, „strahlt weit über die Bedeutung für das Unternehmen hinaus auf die gesamte Stadt aus und wertet den Münchner Norden auf. Mich persönlich", sagte Ude, „begeistert an dem Entwurf die Himmelslandschaft, und mich fasziniert der kommunikative Megaraum,

An early model of the cloudscape: The apparently hovering roof construction of the BMW Welt stands as a symbol of lightness and transparency. Architecture that permits not only open spaces but also open thinking.

To build a cloud that can be walked through on various levels is a grand task. In December 2001 the final decisions were made for the construction of the BMW Welt. One month later its realisation began. Studies arose from sketches, from studies came three-dimensional computer graphics and real hardwood and acrylic-glass architectural models evolved from virtual ones. At the Venice Architecture Biennale 2002, one of these models was showcased in public for the first time. Two miniature video cameras were installed inside the building model. As the model slowly rotated around itself and the two cameras, the video images were projected onto the surrounding walls. They presented perspectives from the inner world of the building and conveyed to the observer the feeling of actually standing inside the BMW Welt. In the meantime, the concept was tirelessly improved upon. The architects construed the centre of the building, the so-called Plaza of the BMW Welt and the largest covered stage of the BMW brand had thereby emerged. Beneath this enormous exhibition-, event- and delivery area, there were initially two, then there came three, then four underground levels: It was necessary to make allowance for an increasing number of services rooms. A total of 1,200 doors within the building today open into more than 1,000 rooms, the majority of them below ground, in the realm of technical services.

Under the sign of technics the enormous 'cloud' roof of the BMW Welt is also to be found. The flat surface construction offered ideal conditions for the installation of photovoltaic equipment that produces eight megawatts of electricity. Within the building the roof's underside evolved, similar to an undulating mountain chain with ceiling heights between eight and twenty metres. Just like an upturned cloudscape, the peaks and troughs recline into the building's interior. The sparkling effect from daylight that refracts through steel girders welded eight thousand times can be observed here on sunny days. This apparently hovering roof construction weighs around 4.000 metric tons and is supported by only eleven slender columns. While high-performance computers were calculating the building's statics, the call for proposals for the building project was begun. BMW assigned the building contract not to a single general contractor, but assigned each project section individually. Contracts were written by the metre. In August 2003, the first excavator arrived on site and initially demolished the former Olympia parking block which then still existed on the site. Later on, hundreds of building workers were busily working here side by side. Auger piles were driven into the ground in order to support the perimeter walls of the so-called 'white bowl', into which the foundations of the BMW Welt were to be poured. Hundreds of tons of earth were excavated from the site and a stream of trucks transported the earth away. In May 2004, the bottom level of the construction pit had been reached: 14 metres deep and covering an area as big as four football pitches. The foundation stone could now be laid. On 16th July 2004 the stone-laying ceremony took place, to which the dignitaries of the City of Munich had been invited. Bavaria's minister-president at that time, Edmund Stoiber, and Munich's lord mayor, Christian Ude, congratulated BMW on their "architectural highlight". The BMW Welt "shines way beyond its significance for the company itself and onto the entire city and enhances the north of Munich", according to the lord mayor. "Personally", said Ude, "what enthrals me about the concept is the skyscape, and the communicative megaspace – which is not committed to a particular aesthetic or a specific use –

Der Himmelsstürmer: Der Wiener Architekt Prof. Wolf D. Prix hat mit seinem visionären Entwurf Architektur- geschichte geschrieben. Das Erreichen der Grubensohle und die Grundsteinlegung sind wichtige Meilensteine in der Baugeschichte der BMW Welt.

der nicht auf eine bestimmte Ästhetik oder eine bestimmte Nutzung festgelegt ist." Noch war nichts zu sehen von diesem „Megaraum". Aber der damalige Vorstandsvorsitzende Dr. Helmut Panke versprach in seiner Rede: „Bald wird die Gestalt der BMW Welt sichtbar werden. Bis zum Richtfest im Frühsommer 2005 werden Hochbau, Stahlkonstruktion, Fassade und Dach fertig gestellt. Die BMW Group investiert über 100 Millionen Euro in die BMW Welt. Insgesamt werden hier circa 200 neue Arbeitsplätze entstehen." „Unsere Architektur", erklärte Prof. Prix, „ist kein modischer Anzug, sondern wie eine Haut, wie eine osmotische Schicht, die Dinge filtert oder durch- lässt. Wir sagen dazu: Das Gefühl des Innen spannt die Haut außen. Sie muss mit den Problemen wachsen, wenn sie gut ist." Prophetische Worte: Die Eröffnung der BMW Welt war für den Sommer 2006 geplant. Eine Hoffnung, die sich bald als unrealistisch erwies. Denn die Schwierigkeiten waren unvermeidbar, was nicht weiter erstaun- lich war bei einem Bauvorhaben in dieser Größenordnung. Der Bau der vier unterirdischen Ebenen ging im Zwei- Schicht-Betrieb noch relativ schnell voran. Am 2. November 2004 wurden auf der untersten Sohle die Fußpunkte für den Doppelkegel gesetzt. Ein Team von BMW Experten koordinierte kontinuierlich 24 Fachbüros und mit ihnen jeden planerischen, konstruktiven und kaufmännischen Schritt. Die Logistik war ein Thema für sich. Auf der Bau- stelle gab es kaum Lagerflächen. Jede Materiallieferung musste nach der Ankunft sofort entladen und verarbei- tet werden. Die Schwertransporter für Fassadenkonstruktionen und die riesigen Dachelemente konnten ihre Ladung nur in den ruhigeren Nachtstunden anliefern, um den regen Stadtverkehr auf den umliegenden Straßen nicht zu stark zu beeinträchtigen.

Im Winter 2004 behinderten große Schneemassen und strenger Frost den Stahlbau. Die Betonarbeiten mussten aus Sicherheitsgründen zwei Wochen ausgesetzt werden. Die Zeit wurde genutzt, um 26 provisorische Rüsttürme aufzustellen, die zunächst das Dach tragen sollten, bevor es auf seine künftigen Stelen abgesenkt wer- den konnte. Für die Konstruktion des Daches fertigten Ingenieure und Bauarbeiter eine obere und eine untere Trägerrostlage. Die dazwischen gesetzten Raumstäbe koppeln die Rasterlagen zu einem räumlichen Tragwerk. Für die 16.000 Quadratmeter große Dachfläche wurden 5.000 Lochbleche aus Edelstahl verwendet. Wegen der Asymmetrie des Daches musste jedes Blech als Einzelstück gefertigt werden. Die Leichtigkeit und Transparenz der Konstruktion garantieren Glasflächen, die beispielsweise im Restaurantbereich oder über der Kundenlounge die Edelstahlbleche ersetzen. Die Dachkonstruktion ist ein Meisterstück der Architektur. Sie schwebt auf 11 fili- granen Betonstützen über der Erlebnislandschaft der BMW Welt. Hier ist das Dach nicht nur Klimaschutz, son- dern ein Raum bildendes Element. In 15 Metern Höhe ist die Kundenlounge angesiedelt, von der aus die Übergabe der jährlich 45.000 neuen BMW Automobile an ihre zukünftigen Besitzer startet. Die spektakuläre Perspektive von der Treppe aus durch das Glasdach in den Himmel dient nicht nur dem Lichteinfall. Sie holt zugleich das BMW Hochhaus optisch in das Gebäude hinein – eine Reverenz des federführenden Architekten der BMW Welt, Prof. Wolf D. Prix, an seinen ehemaligen Lehrer und Mentor Prof. Dr. Karl Schwanzer, der Anfang der 1970er Jahre die Verantwortung für den Bau des Vierzylinders trug. Gleichzeitig mit dem Dach wuchs an der prominentesten Stelle des Areals der aus Stahlfachwerk verschweißte Doppelkegel immer weiter.

High flyer: The Viennese architect Prof. Wolf D. Prix has written architectural history with his visionary concept. Completion of excavation work and laying of the foundation stone are important milestones in the construction history of the BMW Welt.

really fascinates me." There was still nothing yet to be seen of this 'megaspace'. However, the chief executive at that time Dr. Helmut Panke promised in his speech: "The shape of the BMW Welt will very soon be visible. By the time of the topping-out ceremony in the early summer of 2005, the main superstructure, steel construction, facade and roof will have been completed. The BMW Group has invested over 100 million euro in the BMW Welt. A total of about 200 new jobs will be created." "Our architecture", explained Prof. Prix, "is not simply a fashionable new suit, but is like a skin, like an osmotic membrane which filters things out or lets them pass through. What we say is: The internal feeling tenses the outer skin. If it's good enough, it will grow to meet new challenges." Prophetic words: The opening of the BMW Welt was planned for the summer of 2006. A hope that soon proved to be unrealistic. Indeed, the difficulties were inevitable, which was not so surprising with a building project of this magnitude. The construction of the four underground levels in double-shifts progressed relatively rapidly. On 2nd November 2004, the footings for the Double Cone were poured at the lowest excavation level. A team of BMW experts continually coordinated 24 technical offices and every planning, constructional and commercial step concerned with them. The logistics were a subject in itself. There were hardly any storage areas on the building site. Each delivery of materials had to be unloaded and made use of immediately after arrival. The heavy haulage trucks for large parts of the facade construction and the enormous roof elements were able to deliver their loads only in the relatively peaceful hours of the night, in order to not too seriously affect the busy city traffic in the surrounding streets.

In winter 2004 large volumes of snow and severe frost held up steelwork construction. For safety reasons, concrete work had to be postponed for two weeks. The time was used to erect 26 temporary gantries which would initially support the roof before it could be lowered onto its future steles. The engineers and site workers produced an upper and a lower grid raft of girders to facilitate construction of the roof. The spatial rods set between the two rafts connect the grid layers to a spatial load-bearing structure. For the 16,000 square-metre roof area, 5,000 perforated stainless steel panels were used. Due to the asymmetry of the roof, each panel had to be produced individually. The lightness and transparency of the construction is provided by glass surfaces which are used instead of the metal panels for instance in restaurant areas or above the customer lounge. The roof construction is an architectural masterpiece. It hovers on 11 slender concrete pillars, above the 'Event' landscape of the BMW Welt. Here, the roof is not only a building unit affording climate protection, but a space-forming element. The customer lounge, situated 15 metres above the ground, is the place where the process of handing over the new BMW automobiles – 45,000 annually – to their future owners starts. The spectacular perspective from the stairs, through the glass roof up into the sky, serves not only the incidence of light, it also optically brings the BMW tower into the building – a reverential allusion by the leading architect of the BMW Welt, Prof. Wolf D. Prix, to his former tutor and mentor Prof. Dr. Karl Schwanzer who, at the beginning of the 1970s, was responsible for the construction of the BMW four-cylinder. At the same time as the construction of the roof, and at the most prominent position of the site, the welded steel framework Double Cone grew more each day.

Rohbauimpressionen: Zwei Rahmenelemente der tonnenschweren Stahlkonstruktion werden zusammengefügt. Das Gerüst des Doppelkegels und der Verwaltungstrakt der BMW Welt lassen die späteren Formen bereits deutlich erkennen.

Nur auf den ersten Blick den Formen einer Sanduhr nachempfunden, zeigt er bei genauerem Betrachten eine mathematisch wesentlich komplexere Struktur. Als Hauptstütze der gigantischen Dachkonstruktion hat der Doppelkegel nicht nur eine konstruktive Funktion. Dynamisch geschwungen und im Inneren über mehrere Ebenen erschlossen, bildet er den architektonischen Höhepunkt des Gebäudes. Die Fassade des Doppelkegels besteht aus Dreiecksfeldern, die einer vorgegebenen Geometrie folgen. Da die Achse des Doppelkegels geneigt und die Mantelfläche verdreht ist, gleicht keines der aus Stahlrohrprofilen zusammengesetzten Gefache dem anderen. Allein für den Doppelkegel wurden 900 verschiedene Glaselemente gefertigt. Nach oben hin öffnet sich der Kegel zu einem riesigen Trichter, der mit der gewaltigen Bewegung des wolkenartigen Daches verschmilzt – eine statische Höchstleistung.

Die größtenteils gläserne Fassade der BMW Welt kennzeichnet ein Knickriegel, der um das gesamte Gebäude verläuft. Keine Glasscheibe steht hier senkrecht. Das hat nicht nur ästhetische, sondern vor allem bauliche Gründe. Ein so großes Gebäude muss dem Einfluss von Hitze, Kälte oder starkem Wind standhalten und deshalb flexibel sein. Mit diesem Knick werden witterungsbedingte Krafteinwirkungen abgefangen und abgefedert. Bewegungsfugen konnten daher trotz der riesigen Verglasung entfallen. Der Knickriegel verkürzt außerdem die freien Spannweiten der Fassadenträger und minimiert auf diese Weise die Dimensionen der Fassadenprofile. Die auf 15.000 Quadratmetern aus Glaspaneelen bestehende Hauptfassade der BMW Welt trägt das ganze Jahr über zu einer gleich bleibend angenehmen Temperatur im Inneren des Gebäudes bei. Sie sind durch Stahlhohlprofile verbunden, in denen Wasser zirkulieren kann. Im Winter gibt warmes Wasser Wärme nach innen ab. Das verhindert die Bildung von Kondenswasser an den Scheiben. Die Halle der BMW Welt ist natürlich belüftet. Das heißt, das Klima der Halle wird nicht konventionell, sondern über kaltes und warmes Wasser in den Böden reguliert. Um den Energieverbrauch zu minimieren, wurden intensive Berechnungen und Beschattungsstudien erstellt und ein komplexes Lüftungskonzept entwickelt. Das Ergebnis ist eine behagliche Aufenthaltstemperatur, die so wenig Energie wie möglich verbraucht. Warmluft-Aufwärtsströmungen und Warmluftpolster werden im Dach nach außen geführt. Bei Außentemperaturen zwischen 5 und 25 °C öffnen sich Glaselemente in der Fassade und sorgen auf natürlichem Weg für frische Luft. Die Detailplanung und der technische Ausbau benötigten zunehmend Zeit. Im Sommer 2005 war der höchste Punkt der Dachkonstruktion erreicht. Bauherr, Architekten und alle, die am Bau der BMW Welt bisher beteiligt waren, feierten Richtfest. Im Herbst drehten sich riesige Kräne Tag und Nacht über der Baustelle. Deutschlands mächtigster, höchster und mit 500 Tonnen Gewicht schwerster Autokran wurde gebraucht, um einen fast hundert Meter hohen Portalkran mitten aus dem Zentrum der BMW Welt Stück für Stück herauszuheben. Doch auch der strenge Winter 2005 brachte den Zeitplan ins Wanken. Im ganzen Land waren Arbeitskolonnen und sogar das Militär damit beschäftigt, einsturzgefährdete Flachdächer von den Schneemassen zu befreien. Die noch unfertige BMW Welt erlitt keine Schäden, doch die Fertigstellung verschob sich durch die schlechte Witterung erneut. In der Zwischenzeit wurde unter Hochdruck an den nächsten Meilensteinen des Projektes gearbeitet. Die Fertigstellung der äußeren Hülle der BMW Welt war

Impressions of the structural shell: Two framework elements of the heavy steel construction are fitted together. The scaffolding of the Double Cone and the administration tract of the BMW Welt already begin to offer a distinct impression of final forms.

Only at first sight does it appear to be based on the form of an hourglass, but through more precise observation one sees a considerably more complex structure in terms of mathematics. As the main support of the gigantic roof construction, the Double Cone has not only a constructive function. Dynamically swung and connected to various levels in the interior, it forms the architectural highlight of the building. The facade of the Double Cone consists of triangular segments which follow a predetermined geometry. Since the axis of the Double Cone is tilted and the surface area is contorted, none of the steel-pipe-profile elements of the compartmented structure are alike. 900 different glass elements were manufactured for the Double Cone alone. The cone opens upward, forming a giant funnel, fusing with the immense movement of the cloud-like roof – a truly splendid performance from the structure's statics.

The largely glazed facade of the BMW Welt resembles a kinked band running around the entire building. None of the facade's glass panes is vertical. This has not only aesthetic reasons but, above all, structural ones. Such a large building must be able to withstand the effects of heat, cold and strong winds and must therefore be flexible. The effects of forces due to atmospheric conditions are absorbed and cushioned by the facade's kink. Thus, expansion joints were not required despite the enormous dimensions of the glazed surfaces. The kinked band furthermore reduces the free span widths of the facade supports and in this way minimises the dimensions of the facade's lattice profiles. The main facade of the BMW Welt, consisting of 15,000 square metres of glass panels contributes to a constant, comfortable temperature in the interior of the building throughout the year. The glass panels are braced by hollow steel profiles in which water can circulate. In winter, warm water gives off its warmth into the interior. This prevents the build-up of condensation on the panes. The main hall of the BMW Welt is of course ventilated. This means that the air in the hall is not conventionally regulated, but controlled by cold or warm water in the floors. In order to minimise energy consumption, intensive calculations and shading studies were undertaken and a complex ventilation concept was developed. The result is a comfortable habitation temperature that consumes as little energy as possible. Upward currents of warm air and warm air masses are extracted at roof level. With external temperatures of between 5 and 25 °C, glass elements open in the facade and ensure fresh air in a natural way. Detailed planning and technical development required an increase in time expenditure. In the summer of 2005, the highest point in the roof construction had been reached. The clients, architects and all who had up to now taken part in the construction of the BMW Welt celebrated topping-out. In the autumn, giant jib cranes were turning day and night above the building site. Germany's mightiest, tallest and – at 500 metric tons – heaviest truck-mounted crane was required to lift an almost hundred-metre-high gantry crane out of the centre of the BMW Welt piece by piece. Nevertheless, the severe winter of 2005 caused the timetable to be altered. Throughout Germany working gangs and even the military were busy relieving flat roof surfaces – in danger of collapsing – of their masses of snow. The still unfinished BMW Welt suffered no damage, however the completion of construction work was once again delayed due to the bad weather conditions. In the meantime, work continued at full speed on the next milestone

Die Welt zu Füßen: Mit dem Richtfest am 01. Juli 2005 ist der höchste Punkt der Dachkonstruktion erreicht. Zum Start der Fußball-WM im Sommer 2006 erleben Journalisten die BMW Welt von einem Zeppelin aus.

im November 2006 abgeschlossen. Die Fahrzeugaufbereitung im Untergeschoss des Gebäudes wurde im März 2007 funktionsbereit an BMW übergeben. Zur Jahresmitte bezog die Verwaltung der BMW Welt als erste Abteilung ihre Büros. Der Umzug der Mitarbeiter kam früher als erwartet. Denn im baulich hochkomplexen System der BMW Welt erwies sich der Bürotrakt als vergleichsweise unkompliziert und war deshalb frühzeitig fertig gestellt. Im Juli 2007 hatte die Automobilauslieferung in der BMW Welt ihre Premiere. Zunächst waren es BMW Führungskräfte, die hier ihre Dienstwagen übernommen haben – eine interne, aber besonders kritische Kundengruppe. Wer hier zur Abholung kam, war nicht nur Kunde, sondern auch Testperson. Die Eindrücke wurden in Besucherprotokollen vermerkt und später ausgewertet. Auf diese Weise konnte ein möglicher Optimierungsbedarf schnell erkannt und umgesetzt werden. Anfang September konnten sich tausend BMW Mitarbeiter am Standort München über das Intranet in der BMW Welt anmelden. Vier Wochen später waren sie die ersten Besucher, mit denen das Erlebnis- und Auslieferungszentrum seine Funktionalität unter Alltagsbedingungen erprobte. Alle Parketagen waren belegt und dokumentierten damit ihre Betriebsfähigkeit. Informationen in und über die BMW Welt konnten von den Besuchern mühelos gefunden werden. Rund fünfzig Inbetriebnahme-Cluster von den Restaurants bis zu den Aufzügen mussten an diesem Tag erstmals beweisen, dass sie fehlerlos ineinander greifen. Das Haus zeigte an diesem Tag die volle Funktionstüchtigkeit aller Bereiche. Zusätzlich zu den Besucherprotokollen der Gäste berichteten externe Experten zu den Themen Gästebetreuung, gastronomische Betriebe, Informationstransfer und Sicherheit an das Management-Team der BMW Welt und unterstützten dadurch den reibungslosen Betrieb des komplexen Gebäudes.

Ende September tagten erstmals BMW Vertragshändler im Auditorium der BMW Welt und lernten das Gebäude in allen Einzelheiten kennen. Wieder wurden Fragebögen ausgefüllt und ausgewertet, um eine weitere Feinjustierung zu ermöglichen. Anfang Oktober kamen die ersten „Kunden" in die BMW Welt. Die Mitarbeiter der Vertragshändler hatten die Gelegenheit, „ihre" Automobile direkt in der BMW Welt abzuholen um die Eindrücke später unmittelbar weitergeben zu können. Zur feierlichen Eröffnung am 17. Oktober 2007 waren 800 Gäste aus Politik und Gesellschaft eingeladen. Drei Tage später erlaubte es der Tag der offenen Tür den Besuchern auch, Bereiche wie die Premiere oder die Werkstatt zu besichtigen, die eigentlich nur für Kunden oder BMW Mitarbeiter vorgesehen sind. Denn an diesem Tag wurde kein Automobil ausgeliefert. Die BMW Welt selbst war der Star. Am 23. Oktober 2007 startete die reguläre Übergabe der Automobile. Doch immer noch ist für die rund 400 Mitarbeiter der BMW Welt jeder Tag eine neue Herausforderung. Denn täglich geht es darum, die Erwartungen der Kunden und Besucher in der BMW Welt nicht nur zu erfüllen, sondern zu übertreffen.

The world at its feet: With the topping-out ceremony on 1st July 2005, the highest point of the roof construction is reached. At the start of the FIFA World Cup in the summer of 2006, journalists experienced the BMW Welt from aboard a Zeppelin.

of the project. The outer shell of the BMW Welt was completed in November 2006. In March 2007, the vehicle preparation zone in the basement of the building was ready for use and was handed over to BMW. Midway through the year the administration department of the BMW Welt was the first to move into its new offices. The relocation of the employees came sooner than expected. This was because, in the structurally highly complex system of the BMW Welt, the offices tract proved to be comparatively uncomplicated and was therefore completed earlier than expected. In July 2007, automobile delivery in the BMW Welt had its premiere. Initially it was BMW executive personnel who received their new company cars here – an internal, but an especially critical class of customers. Those who came to collect their cars were not only customers but also human test subjects. The impressions were noted in visitor records and later evaluated. In this way, any possible optimisation require-ments could be quickly recognised and implemented. At the beginning of September one thousand BMW employees based in Munich were able, via Intranet, to log-in to the BMW Welt. Four weeks later they were the first visitors with whom the event and delivery centre tested its functionality under everyday conditions. All park-ing levels were full and thereby documented their operating ability. Information in and about the BMW Welt could effortlessly be found by the visitors. On this day, around fifty commissioning computer clusters of services vary-ing from restaurants to the elevators, had to prove for the first time that they were able to faultlessly access each other. During this same day, the building demonstrated the complete operational reliability of all its sectors. In addition to the visitor records, external experts reported to the management team of the BMW Welt on the subjects of looking after visitors, gastronomic services, transfer of information as well as safety and security, thereby contributing to the efficient running of this complex building.

At the end of September appointed BMW dealers held meetings for the first time in the auditorium of the BMW Welt and became acquainted with the building in all its details. Once again, questionnaires were completed and evaluated in order to facilitate a further fine-tuning. At the beginning of October, the first "customers" arrived at the BMW Welt: The appointed dealers' employees had the opportunity to collect "their" automobiles directly from the BMW Welt in order then to be able to immediately pass on their impressions and opinions. At the festive opening ceremony on 17th October 2007, 800 guests were invited including prominent figures from politics and society. Three days later, it was the 'open house' which enabled visitors to look around areas of the building such as the 'Premiere' or the shop floor which are normally only accessed by customers or BMW employees. Indeed, on this day there were no automobile deliveries and the BMW Welt itself was the star attraction. On 23rd October 2007, regular delivery of automobiles began. However, each day is still a new challenge for the 400-or-so employees of the BMW Welt, since every day it is not only a question of fulfilling the expectations of the cus-tomers and visitors of the BMW Welt, but surpassing them.

➤ 78/79 *Abbrucharbeiten: Im August 2003 wird auf dem Gelände der heutigen BMW Welt das BMW Olympia Parkhaus abgerissen.*
Demolition work: In August 2003 on the site of today's BMW Welt, the BMW Olympia parking block is torn down.

➤ 80 *Bewehrungskörbe helfen, die 775 Betonpfeiler der Bohrpfahlwand zu verstärken.*
Steel cage reinforcements facilitate the strengthening of the 775 concrete caisson piles of the bored diaphragm walls.

➤ 81 *Bauvorbereitung: Die jeweils 17 Meter langen Bohrpfähle stützen die Seiten der späteren Baugrube ab.*
Construction preparations: bored piles, each 17 metres long, secure the sides of the construction pit prior to its excavation.

➤ 82/83 *Eine Welt entsteht: 60 Prozent der Gebäudefläche verbergen sich später unter der Erde.*
A world emerges: 60 percent of the floor areas are later hidden underground.

➤ 84 *Flügelglättung im Bereich der Untergeschosse: Knapp 20.000 m³ Beton werden allein für die Bodenplatten verwendet.*
Hover trowelling on the underground levels: Nearly 20,000m³ of concrete is used for the floor slabs alone.

➤ 85 *Eisenflechter bei den Bewehrungsarbeiten: Insgesamt 3,6 Millionen Meter Stabstahl stecken in den Betonkonstruktionen der BMW Welt.*
Steel fixing work on the floor slabs: A total of 3.6 million metres of steel reinforcing rods strengthen the concrete structures of the BMW Welt.

➤ 86/87 *In luftiger Höhe: Von Hubsteigern aus verbinden Fachleute die Stahlbinderelemente für die filigrane Dachkonstruktion der BMW Welt.*
From aerial work platforms: At dizzy heights, specialists join the steel connector components for the intricate roof construction of the BMW Welt.

➤ 88/89 *Der Doppelkegel wird eingerüstet: Ein Wirbelsturm aus Glas und Stahl schraubt sich in den Himmel.*
The Double Cone is scaffolded: A cyclone of glass and steel spirals skyward.

➤ 90/91 *Jeder Handgriff sitzt: Flexarbeiten an den Schweißnähten des Doppelkegels.*
Smooth precision: Angle-grinding work on the weld seams of the Double Cone.

➤ 92/93 *Kulinarischer Ausblick: Der Rohbau des Gastronomiebereiches auf den oberen Ebenen lässt noch nicht an spätere Gaumenfreuden denken.*
Culinary vistas: The shell of the gastronomy sector on the upper levels barely evokes thoughts of delicacies to come.

➤ 94/95 *Die Premiere der BMW Welt: Über die Rampe verlässt der Kunde mit seinem neuen Automobil zukünftig das Erlebnis- und Auslieferungszentrum.*
The centrepiece of the BMW Welt: New owners will leave the event and delivery centre with their automobiles via the exit ramp of the Premiere.

➤ 96/97 *Installation der Drehteller: Auf der Premiere stehen bald die Automobile für die Übergabe bereit.*
Installation of the turntables: Automobiles will soon be placed here in the Premiere ready for their delivery.

➤ 98/99 *Interessante Linienführung: Auskragung des Veranstaltungsbereiches.*
Interesting lineal forms: Cantilevered overhang in the events sector.

➤ 100/101 *Verglasung des Doppelkegels: Jedes Element der Fassade ist ein Einzelstück.*
Glazing of the Double Cone: Each element of the facade is unique.

➤ 102/103 *Nachtimpressionen: Die Baustelle vom BMW Hochhaus aus gesehen.*
Dusk impressions: The building site as seen from the BMW four-cylinder.

➤ 104 *Eine Welt der Technik und Präzision: Regalbediengerät im unterirdischen Tagesspeicher der BMW Welt.*
Technical precision: Test run of the shelving retrieval equipment in the underground car storage of the BMW Welt.

gebaute träume. eine fotografische reise _ building dreams. a photographic journey

gebaute träume. eine fotografische reise _ building dreams. a photographic journey

unter der wolke _ beneath the cloud

Was von außen mit einer faszinierenden Architektur beginnt, findet auch im Inneren seine konsequente Weiterführung. Die Atmosphäre der BMW Welt vermittelt bis ins kleinste Detail den Anspruch des Außergewöhnlichen. Unterschiedliche Raumperspektiven, einfache Orientierung und ein Höchstmaß an Komfort schaffen die Basis für eine lebendige Themenvielfalt rund um Mobilität und Ästhetik. In dieser besonderen Atmosphäre wird mit Hilfe der innovativsten technischen Mittel annähernd das gesamte Spektrum der BMW Produkte präsentiert: Automobile und Motorräder, Zubehör und Dienstleistungen.

The first impression is of the fascinating exterior architecture, and its consistent continuation is to be found within. The atmosphere of the BMW Welt imparts the aspirations of the extraordinary, down to the smallest detail. Diverse spatial perspectives, straightforward orientation and a maximum of comfort create the basis for a lively variety of themes all about mobility and aesthetics. In this special atmosphere and with the help of the most innovative technical means, almost the entire spectrum of BMW products is presented: Automobiles and motorcycles, accessories and services.

Im Herbst 2006 wurden alle Gerüste rund um das Gebäude endgültig abgebaut. In den Musterbüros war die Innenausstattung der BMW Welt längst definiert. Ein Gebäude für Menschen und die Marke BMW entstand. Klare Formen, hochwertige Materialien und reduzierte Farben prägen das Erscheinungsbild. Die Innentopografie schafft auf sechs Ebenen unterschiedlichste Raumdichten und fließende Raumteilungen. Vom Club Restaurant bis zum Erdgeschoss sind die Ebenen der BMW Welt optisch miteinander verbunden. Es sind offene Räume – voneinander abgegrenzt, aber nicht zwangsläufig voneinander getrennt. Es herrschen Ordnung und Übersicht. Jeder weiß zu jeder Zeit, wo er sich befindet. Die Marke BMW hat viele Facetten. Und jede von ihnen wird in der BMW Welt spürbar. Der avantgardistische Doppelkegel ist der beste Ort, um eine Reise durch die BMW Welt zu beginnen. Er ist der architektonisch-kommunikative Ursprung des Gebäudes. Durch die exponierte Lage und seine optische Besonderheit ist der Doppelkegel die ideale Plattform für Ausstellungen rund um Marke und Produkte sowie für Veranstaltungen aus den Bereichen Wirtschaft, Politik, Technologie, Gesellschaft, Kunst und Kultur. Aktuelle BMW Themen werden hier in glanzvollem Licht präsentiert. Eine drehbare Bühne rückt das Highlight eines jeden Events in die richtige Position. Während im Erdgeschoss die Produktausstellung im Vordergrund steht, bietet das Untergeschoss mit seiner loungeähnlichen Atmosphäre die Gelegenheit zum entspannten Vertiefen der jeweiligen Ausstellungsthemen. In einem stilvollen Ambiente aus erstklassigem Design und emotionaler Lichtinszenierung werden Veranstaltungen aller Art zum Erlebnis. Interaktiv-Tische laden zur Auseinandersetzung mit Produkt- und Markenthemen ein. Ein faszinierendes Raumerlebnis und den besten Blick auf das Geschehen hat man von der freitragenden Wendeltreppe aus. Sie führt an der Fassade des Doppelkegels vom Erdgeschoss bis an die schmalste Stelle der Konstruktion. Durch die 60 Monitore entlang der Wendeltreppe wird aus dem Doppelkegel ein medialer Dom aus Licht und Ton.

Am oberen Ende der Wendeltreppe entlässt der Doppelkegel den Besucher auf die Galerie. Diese Brücke verbindet Museum und Werkgelände in siebeneinhalb Metern Höhe mit der BMW Welt. Wie eine Welle durchfließt sie das Gebäude von Süden nach Norden. Drei Inseln laden auf der Galerie zum Verweilen ein. Sie ermöglichen es dem Besucher, die Inszenierung der Marke auf sich wirken zu lassen. Von diesem Standpunkt ist die Premiere gut zu sehen, die weltweit größte Bühne für die Auslieferung von BMW Automobilen. Auf 20 Drehtellern und zehn Panoramaplätzen stehen die neuen Fahrzeuge für ihre Besitzer bereit. Von der Galerie aus eröffnen sich noch weitere eindrucksvolle Perspektiven. In der Halle, der so genannten Plaza, präsentiert sich die Automobilausstellung. Auf 120 Metern Länge wird hier die aktuelle Produktpalette, von der Limousine über den Roadster, das Cabriolet oder den Touring bis zum „Sports Activity Vehicle" gezeigt. Ebenfalls im Blickfeld sind die Kundenlounges, die den Abholern am Tag der Automobilauslieferung zur Verfügung stehen. Hier warten die zukünftigen Besitzer darauf, den Schlüssel zu ihrem Fahrzeug in Empfang zu nehmen. Doch zuvor werden sie von ihrem Kundenbetreuer im Produkt Info Center über die faszinierenden Details ihres neuen Automobils informiert. Der in Weiß, Schwarz, Grau und Silber gehaltene High-Tech-Raum bietet eine faszinierende Kulisse, um die verborgenen Qualitäten eines BMW zu kommunizieren. Denn jeder Kunde soll von Anfang an die beruhigende

In the autumn of 2006 all of the scaffolding right around the building was finally dismantled. In the model offices, the interiors of the BMW Welt had long been defined. A building for people and for the BMW brand arose. Clear forms, high quality materials and subtle colours shape the overall appearance. The interior topography creates the most varying spatial volumes and allows flowing space allocation on six levels. From the Club Restaurant to the ground floor, the levels of the BMW Welt are optically connected to one another. They are open spaces – delimited between them but not necessarily separated from each other. Order and a clear perspective prevail. At any time you know where you are. The BMW brand has many facets, and each one of them is perceptible in the BMW Welt. The avantgarde Double Cone is the best place to begin an excursion through the BMW Welt. It is the architecturally communicative source of the building. Due to its prominent location and its visual distinctiveness, the Double Cone is the ideal environment for staging exhibitions all about the brand and its products, and for events in the fields of economy, politics, technology, society, art and culture. Current BMW themes are presented here in a splendidly illuminated setting. A revolvable stage draws the highlight of each event into the right position. Whereas the product exhibition comes to the fore on the ground floor, the lower level with its lounge-like atmosphere offers the opportunity to relaxingly delve into each individual exhibition theme. In a stylish ambience of first class design and an emotionally sculptured use of light, events of all varieties become moving experiences. Interactive consoles invite you to examine product and brand topics. A fascinating spatial experience and excellent views of all the activities can best be achieved from the free-standing spiral staircase. It runs along the interior of the Double Cone's facade from the ground floor to the narrowest point of the construction. Due to the 60 monitors along the length of the spiral staircase, the Double Cone becomes a medial dome of light and sound.

At the top end of the spiral staircase the Double Cone leads the visitor onto the gallery. This bridge links the museum and the home plant with the BMW Welt at a height of seven and a half metres. Just like a wave, it flows through the building from south to north. Three isles invite you to linger a while on the gallery. They facilitate the staging of the brand to take its effect on the visitor. From this position the Premiere can be seen clearly, the world's largest stage for delivery of BMW automobiles. On 20 turntables and in ten panorama spaces, new vehicles stand ready for their future owners. When viewed from the gallery, further impressive perspectives are opened up. In the main hall, the so-called Plaza, the automobile exhibition is presented. Spread out over 120 metres, the current product range is displayed, including sedans, roadsters, convertibles and touring cars, as well as Sports Activity Vehicles. Equally well visible from the gallery are the customer lounges, which are available to the customers on the day of their automobile delivery. It is here that future owners wait to receive the keys to their vehicles. However, before this their BMW assistants inform them in the Product Info Center about the fascinating details of their new automobiles. This high-tech area, designed in black, white, grey and silver, provides a fascinating setting for communicating the hidden qualities of a BMW. Indeed, from the very beginning every customer should come to know with reassuring certainty that his vehicle offers not only ideal dynamics and comfort, but also ideal safety characteristics. On one of the 16 Info Tables the automobile that the customer will later collect

Gewissheit erfahren, dass sein Fahrzeug nicht nur ein Optimum an Dynamik und Komfort, sondern auch an Sicherheit bietet. Auf einem der 16 Info-Tische wird exakt das Automobil abgebildet, das der Kunde später abholen wird. Jedes Detail der virtuellen Animation ist authentisch, von der Ausstattung bis zum Nummernschild. Mehr als 200 Briefings sind täglich im Produkt Info Center möglich. Damit sich Kunden- und Betreuer-Teams dabei nicht gegenseitig stören, ist der Raum perfekt schallgedämpft. Sensoren messen ständig den Geräuschpegel und sorgen nach Bedarf für ein unauffälliges Hintergrundrauschen, das die Gespräche an den benachbarten Stationen angenehm abschwächt. Im Produkt Info Center werden alle Sinne angesprochen. Am Wirkungsexponat wird über Klangbeispiele auf die Wahrnehmung von Qualität eingegangen. Im Info Modul, einer Art Fahrsimulator, kann sich der neue Besitzer mit den hochwertigen technischen Besonderheiten seines Fahrzeuges vertraut machen, die in vielen Fällen auf elektronischen Regelsystemen beruhen.

Auf der Galerie führt der Weg weiter vorbei am Restaurant International, am BMW Welt Shop und der Coffee Bar. Von hier aus sind auch das Club Restaurant und der Business Club zu sehen, die eine Ebene höher unter dem Dach der BMW Welt ihren exponierten und gleichzeitig unaufdringlichen Platz einnehmen. Wie überall in der BMW Welt prägen formvollendete Eleganz und klares Design das Ambiente. Für das Mobiliar gelten strenge Formen, die durch hochwertige Materialien wie Glas, Edelstahl und Marmor veredelt werden. Im Restaurant International harmoniert die Gestaltung mit dem Fußboden aus gekalkter Eiche im Inneren und ausgewählten Hölzern auf der sich zum Olympiapark öffnenden Terrasse. In der einsehbaren Schauküche entfalten bis zu acht Köche gleichzeitig ihre kulinarischen Raffinessen. „Please wait to be seated" heißt es nach internationalem Standard eine Ebene weiter oben im exklusiven Club Restaurant. Wer nicht sofort an seinem Tisch Platz nehmen möchte, hat im Lounge-Bereich die Möglichkeit zum Aperitif, entweder an der Bar oder in einer der bequemen Sitzgruppen. Die Restaurantbereiche sind durch unterleuchtete Stufen gekennzeichnet – auch hier betonen und gliedern Lichtleisten den Raum. Tischlampen und Kerzen erzeugen eine angenehme Atmosphäre. Das Club Restaurant verfügt über 50, der benachbarte Business Club über weitere 20 Plätze. Mittelpunkt des Club Restaurants ist die nach allen Seiten offene Kochbühne. Hier gewähren Spitzenköche aus aller Welt Einblicke in ihre Kunst und bereiten am frei stehenden Molteni-Gussherd exquisite Gerichte zu. Die Menüs werden jeden Tag neu zusammengestellt – bestellt wird à la carte oder direkt beim Koch, der gerne über die tagesaktuellen Spezialitäten informiert. Vielfalt und Abwechslung auf hohem Niveau, so lautet hier das Prinzip. Der Weinschrank im Lounge-Bereich des Restaurants wartet mit erlesenen Tropfen auf den wahren Connaisseur. Die besondere Ausstattung des Club Restaurants entspricht seinem edlen Charakter: Der Bodenbelag ist aus amerikanischem Walnussholz gefertigt. Im Bereich der Bar wurde schwarzer Granit verwendet, einzelne Wände sind mit edlem Samt bespannt. Ein besonderer Marmor verbindet den Service- mit dem Gästebereich. Die Homogenität von Design und Funktionalität wird im Restaurant durch Drehstühle dokumentiert. Sie ermöglichen es dem Besucher, sich bequem vom Tisch weg der großen Glasfront zuzuwenden, durch die man auf die Premiere und in die Plaza hinunterschauen kann.

is exactly reproduced. Every detail of the virtual animation is authentic, from the furnishings and extras, to the number plate. More than 200 briefings are possible each day in the Product Info Center. In order to prevent the assistant-and-customer dialogues from disturbing each other, the area is perfectly designed for noise-reduction. Sensors continually measure noise levels and, as required, provide for an unobtrusive background sound that pleasantly attenuates the conversations at the neighbouring consoles. In the Product Info Center all of one's senses are addressed. At the Effects exhibit the perception of quality can be looked into via examples of sound. In the Info Module, a kind of driving simulator, the new owner can familiarise himself with the high-grade technical particulars of his vehicle, which in many cases are based on electronic regulating systems.

Further along the gallery, the route passes the Restaurant International, the BMW Welt Shop and the Coffee Bar. The Club Restaurant and the Business Club can also be seen from here. They are situated one level higher, under the roof of the BMW Welt at a prominent and at the same time unobtrusive location. As everywhere else in the BMW Welt, elegance and clear design characterise the ambience. Strict forms are complied with for the furnishings, which are further refined by use of high-grade materials such as glass, stainless steel and marble. In the Restaurant International the design harmonises with limed oak flooring in the interior and selected woods on the terrace that opens onto the Olympic Park. In the well-displayed, open-view kitchen as many as eight cooks simultaneously unfurl their culinary finesse. 'Please wait to be seated' is, according to international standards, the maxim in the Club Restaurant one level higher. Whoever desires to take his place at table a little later, has the possibility to take an aperitif in the lounge area, either at the bar or in one of the comfortable lounge suites. Uplit steps denote the restaurant areas – and strip lights articulate and accentuate the areas here also. Table lamps and candles create a pleasant atmosphere. The exclusive Club Restaurant has places for over 50 guests at its disposal, and the neighbouring Business Club has a further 20. The centre-piece of both restaurants is a cooking stage open on three sides. Chefs from all over the world afford glimpses into their art and prepare exquisite dishes at the free-standing cast iron Molteni stove. The menus are compiled new each day – ordering is à la carte or directly from the cook, who is happy to inform you about the day's current specialities. The principle here is variety and diversification of a high standard. The wine cabinet in the lounge area of the restaurant awaits the veritable connoisseur with its carefully selected delights. The special décor of the Club Restaurant reflects its distinguished character: The flooring surfaces are of American black walnut. In the area around the bar, black granite has been chosen, and some of the walls are covered with fine velvet. An exceptional variety of marble links the service and guest areas. The homogeneity of design and functionality is demonstrated via swivel chairs in the restaurant. They enable the visitor to comfortably turn away from the table and towards the large glass front, through which one can look down onto the Premiere and into the Plaza.

The Coffee Bar on the same level as the Restaurant International directly beside the BMW Welt Shop is designed in a U-form. As in all of the gastronomy areas, the furnishings include integrated light elements. The

Die Coffee Bar auf der Ebene des Restaurants International direkt neben dem BMW Welt Shop ist in U-Form gestaltet. Wie überall in den Gastronomiebereichen sind in das Mobiliar Lichtelemente integriert. Die Illumination der Einrichtung ist Designelement und taucht den Raum gleichzeitig in ein warmes Licht. In der Coffee Bar wird der Kaffee nicht mit gewöhnlichen Kaffeevollautomaten zubereitet. Die Bohnen werden von Meistern ihres Faches frisch gemahlen und in exklusiven Geräten mit hohem Druck aufgebrüht. Wer Tee bevorzugt, kann sich verschiedene Sorten mit heißem Wasser aus dem Samowar servieren lassen. Von frisch gepressten Säften bis zum frozen coffee reicht die Auswahl an kalten Getränken. Die passende Lektüre zum Kaffee bietet der benachbarte BMW Welt Shop. Hier können nicht nur internationale Tageszeitungen und Lifestylemagazine erworben werden. Aktuelle Publikationen zu BMW Automobilen, aber auch zu Themen wie Architektur und Design liefern spannende und unterhaltsame Informationen. Passende Souvenirs zur Erinnerung an den ereignisreichen Tag sind im Bereich BMW Welt Merchandising zu finden.

In der Verlängerung der Galerie hat die Freiheit auf zwei Rädern ihren Platz gefunden. Dieser Teil der Ausstellungsfläche widmet sich den BMW Motorrädern. Hier werden Zweiräder präsentiert, von geländegängigen Enduros über große Tourer bis hin zu City Bikes. Mediale Inszenierungen führen in die Erlebniswelt des Motorradfahrens ein. Auch das umfangreiche Sortiment an Zubehör und Accessoires kann man in diesem Bereich der BMW Welt kennenlernen. Auf gleicher Ebene befindet sich das Business Center, das über zwei räumlich flexible und technisch perfekt ausgestattete Tagungsräume sowie ein großzügiges Foyer verfügt. Die individuellen Wünsche der Gäste bestimmen hier die modulare Raumgestaltung und den Einsatz modernster Medien- und Konferenztechnik. Zum Business Center gehören eine Innen- sowie eine Außenterrasse. Es ist ebenso wie das Auditorium dem Veranstaltungsforum der BMW Welt angegliedert. Eine Treppe führt von der Motorradausstellung hinunter zum Foyer des Auditoriums, dem multifunktionellen Veranstaltungssaal der BMW Welt. Separate Bodenelemente ermöglichen eine flexible Höhenjustierung und erlauben dadurch unterschiedliche Eventkonzepte. Vom Kongress über Bankette und Kinovorführungen bis zum musikalischen Live-Auftritt werden hier auf 945 Quadratmetern alle technischen Register gezogen, um den Begriff Raum immer wieder neu zu interpretieren. Ein 16 Tonnen schweres, vollständig im Boden versenkbares Hubtor macht es möglich, das komplette Auditorium auch als offenes Forum zu nutzen. Gegenüber dem Veranstaltungsforum und dem Eingang Nord haben die Besucher der BMW Welt im Bistro die Möglichkeit, sich mit kleinen, unkomplizierten Gerichten zu stärken. „Quick and easy" heißt das Konzept. Bereits ab sieben Uhr morgens wird hier Frühstück serviert. Das reichhaltige Angebot an Erfrischungen und Snacks wechselt mit der Tageszeit. Die nur durch eine Glasscheibe vom Bistro getrennte Bäckerei liefert für alle Restaurants der BMW Welt ständig eine Vielzahl frischer Brot- und Gebäcksorten. Wie in allen Gastronomiebereichen dominieren auch im Bistro die prägenden architektonischen Elemente Stahl und Glas. Die Stühle sind mit einem speziellen Leder aus der BMW Individual-Kollektion bezogen. Die ungewöhnliche Höhe der von innen beleuchteten Tische und der Stühle weicht nach oben von der Norm ab und garantiert so den perfekten Überblick.

illumination of the fittings is a design element and at the same time it immerses the area in a warm light. The coffee served in the Coffee Bar is not prepared with conventional, fully automatic coffee machines – the beans are freshly ground by experts in their trade and then each serving is made in exclusive high-pressure appliances. Whoever prefers tea will find it in a variety of blends and can have it served with hot water from the samovar. The selection of cold drinks ranges from freshly squeezed juices to frozen coffee. Suitable reading material for a coffee break is offered in the neighbouring BMW Welt Shop. Not only international daily newspapers and lifestyle magazines can be found here but also current publications on BMW automobiles as well as on themes such as architecture and design offer exciting and entertaining information. Suitable souvenirs to recall the eventful day are to be found in the BMW Welt Merchandising section.

In the extension of the gallery, freedom on two wheels has found a home. This part of the exhibition area is dedicated to BMW motorcycles. Two-wheelers are presented here, from all-terrain enduros to grand tourer bikes to city bikes. Medial staging provides an interesting introduction to the motorbike-riding world of experience. Furthermore, one can become acquainted with the comprehensive selection of equipment and accessories in this area of the BMW Welt. On the same level the Business Center is to be found, which includes two spatially flexible and technically perfect conference rooms as well as an extensive foyer. The individual wishes of the visitors determine here the modular spatial configuration and the application of state-of-the-art media and conference technology. An internal and an external terrace are also part of the Business Center, and just as with the Auditorium, it is also connected to the Event Forum of the BMW Welt. A stairway leads from the motorcycle exhibition down to the foyer of the auditorium, the multifunctional event hall of the BMW Welt. Separate floor elements facilitate flexible height adjustment and thus enable varying event concepts. From congresses and banquets to film presentations and musical live performances, the staff here can pull out all the technical stops on 945 square metres of floor space to frequently reinterpret the term 'setting'. A 16 tonne lift gate that can be completely submerged into the floor makes it possible to use the entire auditorium as an open forum as well. Opposite the Event Forum and the northern entrance, visitors to the BMW Welt have the opportunity to enjoy a meal in the Bistro, where small, uncomplicated dishes are offered. 'Quick and easy' is the motto here, and breakfast is served from as early as seven o'clock in the mornings. The rich selection of refreshments and snacks changes with the time of day. The bakery, separated from the Bistro only by a glass screen, continually delivers a wide variety of fresh bread and pastries for all of the restaurants in the BMW Welt. As in all other gastronomic areas, the impressive architectural elements of steel and glass dominate here in the Bistro as well. The chairs are covered with special leather from the BMW Individual Collection. The unusual height of the tables – illuminated from within – and of the chairs differs from the norm, being somewhat higher, thus ensuring a perfect overview.

Beneath a glass plate in the floor prominently placed at the northern entrance lies the foundation stone of the BMW Welt. To the right, the open way leads the visitor from north to south across the Plaza. Here in the

Unter einer Glasplatte im Boden am Eingang Nord liegt prominent platziert der Grundstein der BMW Welt. Rechts entlang führt der Weg den Besucher von Norden nach Süden über die Plaza. Hier in der Automobilpräsentation zeigen sich die aktuellen BMW Automobile ganz aus der Nähe, während die Galerie einen beeindruckenden Gesamtüberblick auf die Produktpalette ermöglicht. Im Zentrum der Plaza und damit im Herzen der BMW Welt liegt das Technik und Design Atelier. Hier werden die technische Innovationskraft und das emotionale Design der Marke BMW aktiv und interaktiv erlebbar. Technik und Design zum Fühlen, Sehen und Hören. BMW EfficientDynamics steht im Mittelpunkt des Technikbereiches und zeigt, dass sich Freude am Fahren und Umweltverantwortung nicht gegenseitig ausschließen. Hier können Themen wie Motoroptimierung, Bremsenergierückgewinnung oder die Auto Start Stop Funktion entdeckt werden, durch die BMW die Fahrfreude weiter ausbaut – mit mehr Leistung und weniger Verbrauch. Als Meilenstein auf dem Weg zu einer nachhaltigen und schadstofffreien Mobilität wird der Hydrogen 7, das erste Serienfahrzeug mit Wasserstoffantrieb, im Bereich BMW CleanEnergy vorgestellt. Die sprichwörtliche BMW Motorenkompetenz, BMW xDrive, die neuesten Fahrerassistenzsysteme oder BMW ConnectedDrive erleben die Besucher im Technik und Design Atelier. Hier erfahren sie auch mehr über die BMW Designphilosophie, das Interieur und Exterieur der BMW Automobile und den Designkonfigurator.

An die Automobilpräsentation auf der Plaza schließt sich ein verglaster Raum mit einer komfortablen Lounge an. BMW Individual zeigt hier neben zwei unterschiedlich ausgestatteten Fahrzeugen eine sieben Meter lange Musterwand mit vielfältigen Farben und Materialien wie seltenen Hölzern, ungewöhnlich verarbeiteten Lederarten und besonderen Lacken. An BMW Individual grenzt der Junior Campus, der dem Nachwuchs eine spannende Erlebniswelt zum Thema Mobilität eröffnet. „Mobilität mit allen Sinnen entdecken" ist das Konzept des Bereiches, der in Zusammenarbeit mit renommierten Pädagogen und Wissenschaftlern entstanden ist. Ein einzigartiger Ort, an dem zugleich Fantasie und Neugier gefördert sowie technisches Wissen vermittelt wird. Der Junior Campus besteht aus drei Erlebnisräumen. Das Campus Portal ist für Besucher jedes Alters frei zugänglich. Hier kann man auf eigene Faust erkunden, was sich hinter dem Begriff „Mobilität" verbirgt. Die Attraktion des Campus Portals ist die große gläserne Kugelbahn. Auf verschlungenen Wegen, über elegante Kurven, Loopings und Geraden bringt man die Kugel ins Ziel. Wer den Dingen gerne auf den Grund geht, begegnet in diesem Raum einem echten Traumwagen. Mit den flexiblen Monitoren, die sich über das ganze Fahrzeug bewegen lassen, kann der Besucher viele spannende Themen, die sich hinter dem Begriff Mobilität verstecken, für sich entdecken. Im Campus Labor und in der Campus Werkstatt finden vertiefende Workshops für Kinder und Jugendliche im Alter von 7 bis 13 Jahren statt. Hier testen die jungen Ingenieure unterschiedliche Radaufhängungen und lernen deren Unterschiede kennen. Sie finden heraus, wie Kräfte beherrscht werden können, wie man die Explosionskraft lenkt und in Bewegung verwandelt und mit welchen Energien man heute und in Zukunft Fahrzeuge antreibt. Zum Abschluss testet ein Quiz das erworbene Wissen aus den Themenbereichen Energie, Umwelt, Antrieb und Sicherheit oder Verkehr. In der Campus Werkstatt erhalten die jungen Besucher den Auftrag,

automobile presentation area the product range of current BMW automobiles is perceived 'right up close', while the gallery offers an impressive general overview across the product range. In the centre of the Plaza and thus at the heart of the BMW Welt is the Technology and Design Atelier. The technically innovative strength and the BMW brand's emotional design is an actively and interactively tangible experience. Technology and design to be touched, seen and heard. BMW EfficientDynamics stands at the centre of the technology area and demonstrates that sheer driving pleasure and responsibility for the environment are not mutually exclusive. Topics such as motor optimisation, brake energy recovery or the Auto Start Stop function can be discovered here, through which BMW further develop the joy of driving – with more performance and less wastage. As a milestone on the way to a sustainable and pollution-free mobility, the Hydrogen 7 is introduced in the BMW CleanEnergy area, the first ever hydrogen-powered production vehicle. Visitors can experience the proverbial BMW motor competence, BMW xDrive, the latest driver assistance systems or BMW ConnectedDrive in the Technology and Design Atelier. Here they will also experience more about BMW's design philosophy, the interior and exterior of BMW automobiles and the design configurator.

At the automobile presentation in the Plaza, a glazed space is linked to a comfortable lounge. BMW Individual displays here, along with two vehicles equipped in different ways, a seven metre long wall of samples with many varying colours and materials such as rare woods, unusually processed kinds of leather and special paints. BMW Individual borders onto the Junior Campus, which opens up an exciting world of experience to young talent on the theme of mobility. 'Discover mobility with all your senses' is the concept of this area that has arisen in collaboration with well-known educators and scientists. A unique place where both imagination and curiosity are encouraged and where technical knowledge is passed on at the same time. The Junior Campus consists of three realms of experience. The Campus Portal is freely accessible to visitors of all ages. One can investigate here on one's own initiative that which is concealed in the term 'mobility'. The Campus Portal's main attraction is the big glass rolling ball track. Along serpentine lanes, and via elegant curves, loops and straights, the marbles eventually roll down to the finish. Those who prefer to look deeper into things will discover a real dream car in this room. By using moveable monitors, which can be pushed across the entire vehicle, the visitor can discover the many exciting topics that the subject of mobility has to offer. In the Campus Laboratory and in the Campus Workshop more profound workshop-seminars for children and young people from 7 to 13 years old take place. The young engineers test here various wheel suspension mountings and learn about their differences. They find out how various forces can be controlled, how explosive combustion forces are channelled and converted into movement. They also discover which energies drive vehicles of today and of the future. On completion, a quiz tests the newly acquired knowledge of such subjects as energy, environment, drive and safety or road traffic. Young visitors to the Campus Workshop are given the task of building a vehicle together. The best models are then exhibited on the conveyor belt that runs through the rooms of the Junior Campus. On completion each workshop-seminar participant receives a diploma. Directly beside the Junior Campus, the world's largest BMW

gemeinsam ein Fahrzeug zu bauen. Die besten Modelle werden schließlich in der Förderstraße ausgestellt, die durch die Räume des Junior Campus führt. Zum Abschluss erhält jeder, der an diesen Workshops teilgenommen hat, ein Diplom. Direkt neben dem Junior Campus befindet sich der weltweit größte BMW Lifestyle Shop. Hier erwartet den Besucher auf zwei Ebenen die komplette Auswahl aller BMW Artikel aus dem Lifestylebereich. Ebenfalls erhältlich ist das gesamte Sortiment der Sponsoringwelt von BMW: Golf, Segeln und Formel 1. Das Angebot reicht vom hochwertigen Reisegepäck über Fahrräder und Baby Racer bis hin zu Funktionsbekleidung und Accessoires.

Am Südeingang, direkt neben dem Doppelkegel, findet der Rundgang durch die BMW Welt sein Ende. Von den insgesamt neun Geschossen befinden sich vier unter der Erde. Die Gesamtfläche des Gebäudes umfasst zehn Fußballfelder und mehr als 1.000 Räume. Doch für die meisten Besucher ist nur ein kleiner Teil zugänglich. Im Tagesspeicher warten 284 neue Automobile auf ihren Auftritt im Rampenlicht der Premiere. Die Fahrzeuge stehen hier in der sicheren Welt von Elektronik und Präzision. Menschen haben keinen Zutritt. Aus Brandschutzgründen ist der Sauerstoffgehalt reduziert. Deshalb lässt sich die Maßarbeit der computergesteuerten Regalbediengeräte nur durch ein Sichtfenster beobachten. Für die Automobilübergabe werden die neuen Fahrzeuge im gläsernen Aufzug über drei Ebenen auf die Premiere transportiert. Unter dem Doppelkegel arbeiten Fachkräfte in der Fahrzeugvorbereitung der BMW Welt. Sie bereiten die neuen Automobile auf und prüfen vor der Übergabe ein letztes Mal sämtliche Funktionen. In einer 40 Meter langen Waschstraße wird jeder BMW auf Hochglanz gebracht. Nach neuesten Umweltschutzrichtlinien wird das Waschwasser biologisch aufbereitet und lässt sich dadurch wieder verwerten. Eine zentrale Staubsaugeranlage sorgt für eine letzte gründliche Reinigung. Denn zur Premiere muss das Automobil makellos sein. In anderen Kellerbereichen arbeiten Wärme- und Kältemaschinen. Ihre Heizleistung könnte 250 Einfamilienhäuser temperieren, ihre Kälteleistung 25.000 Haushaltskühlschränke betreiben. Die Gebäudetechnik beansprucht in den Kellergeschossen 8.000 Quadratmeter. Ein anderer erheblicher Teil wird für die Tiefgarage mit 584 Stellplätzen genutzt. Jeder Raum der BMW Welt muss nicht nur für sich selbst, sondern auch im Zusammenspiel mit allen anderen Bereichen das leisten, wozu er konzipiert und eingerichtet wurde. Von der Werkstatt bis zur Automobilübergabe greifen hier komplexe Strukturen gekonnt ineinander. Sie garantieren die reibungslose Inszenierung, die der Besucher als einen perfekten Tag in der BMW Welt erlebt. Dieser scheinbar mühelose Ablauf ist nicht nur das Ergebnis einer durchdachten Konzeption und detaillierten Planung. Ein mehrmonatiger Testlauf vor der großen Eröffnung hat Aufschluss darüber gegeben, wie die BMW Welt unter realen Bedingungen tatsächlich funktioniert.

Lifestyle Shop is to be found. Here on two levels the entire selection of all BMW articles from the realm of lifestyle awaits the visitor. The complete product range from the sponsoring world of BMW – golf, sailing and Formula 1 – is also available. The choice of products ranges from high-end luggage to bicycles and Baby Racers, to technical apparel and accessories.

At the southern entrance directly beside the Double Cone, the walk around the BMW Welt comes to an end. From a total of nine levels, four are to be found underground. The total floor area of the building equals that of ten football pitches and more than 1,000 rooms. However, only a small number of them are accessible for the majority of visitors. In the car storage, 284 new automobiles await their entry into the limelight of the Premiere. The vehicles are stored here in the secure world of electronics and precision, people are not allowed access: The oxygen content in these rooms is reduced for fire prevention, and this is why the precision work of the computer-controlled racking storage and retrieval system can only be observed through a viewing panel. The new vehicles are lifted through three levels by a glass elevator onto the Premiere for the automobile delivery. Beneath the Double Cone skilled personnel work in the BMW Welt's vehicle preparation. They process the new automobiles and examine all functions one final time before they are handed over. In a 40 metre long carwash each BMW is cleaned and polished to a high finish. In accordance with current environmental protection policies, the used water is biologically treated and is thus able to be reused. A central vacuum cleaning installation provides a final thorough cleaning. Indeed, for the Premiere the automobile must be spotlessly clean. In other underground areas heating and cooling equipment is in operation whose heat output could supply 250 single-family houses, and whose cooling capacity equals 25,000 household refrigerators. The building services engineering takes up 8,000 square metres of the underground levels. Another considerable part of this area is used up by the underground parking lot with 584 spaces. Each room in the BMW Welt has to serve not only its own functions but must also interact with all other areas and provide the services for which it has been conceived and constructed. From workshop to automobile delivery, complex structures skilfully interact here with each other. They ensure the smooth staging and presentation that the visitor experiences as a perfect day in the BMW Welt. This apparently effortless process is not only the result of a thought-out conception and detailed planning. A test run lasting many months that took place before the grand opening demonstrated in which way the BMW Welt would actually function under real conditions.

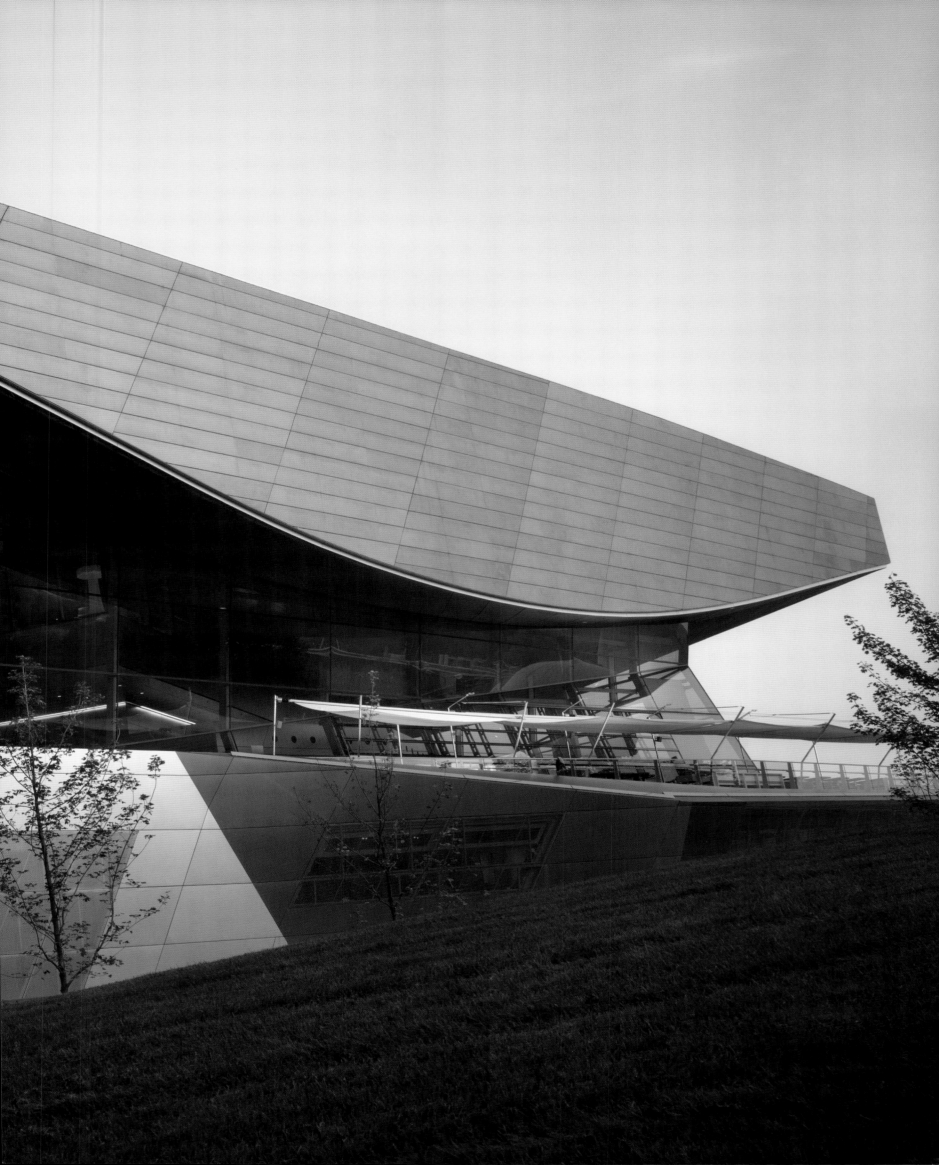

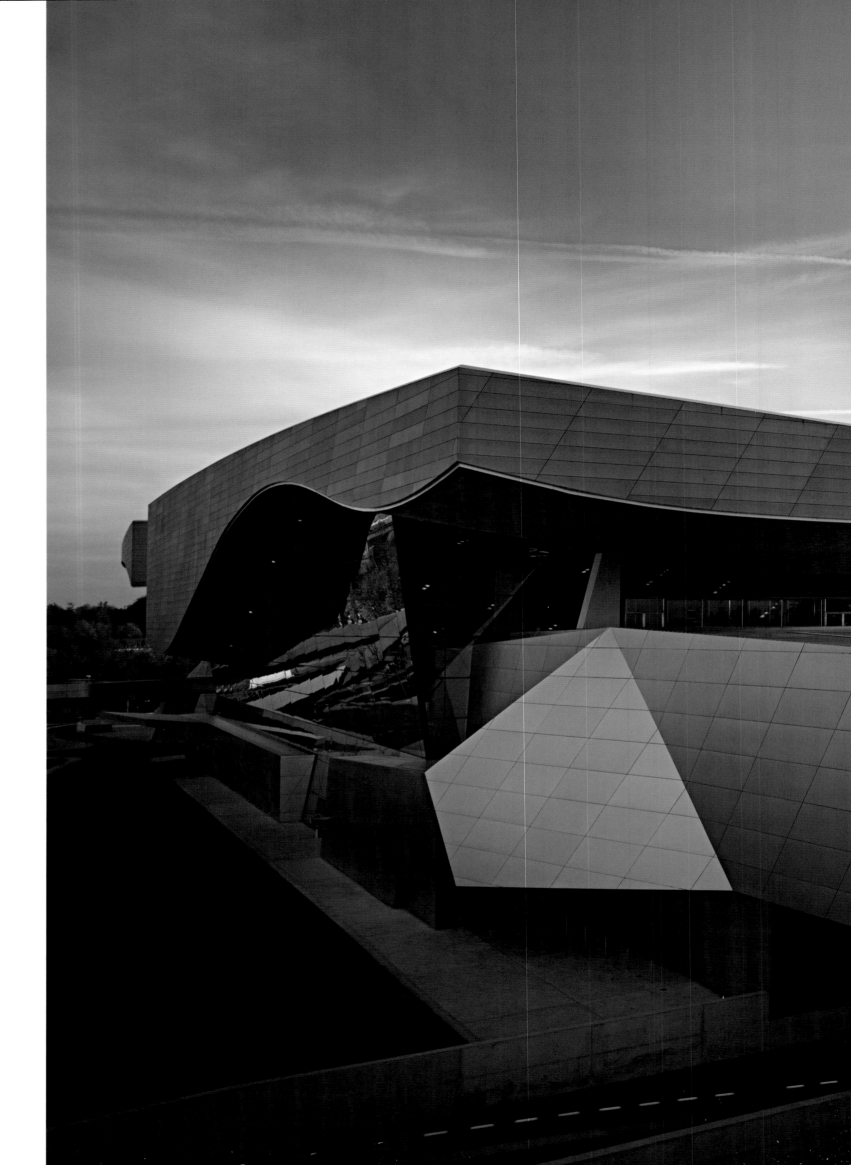

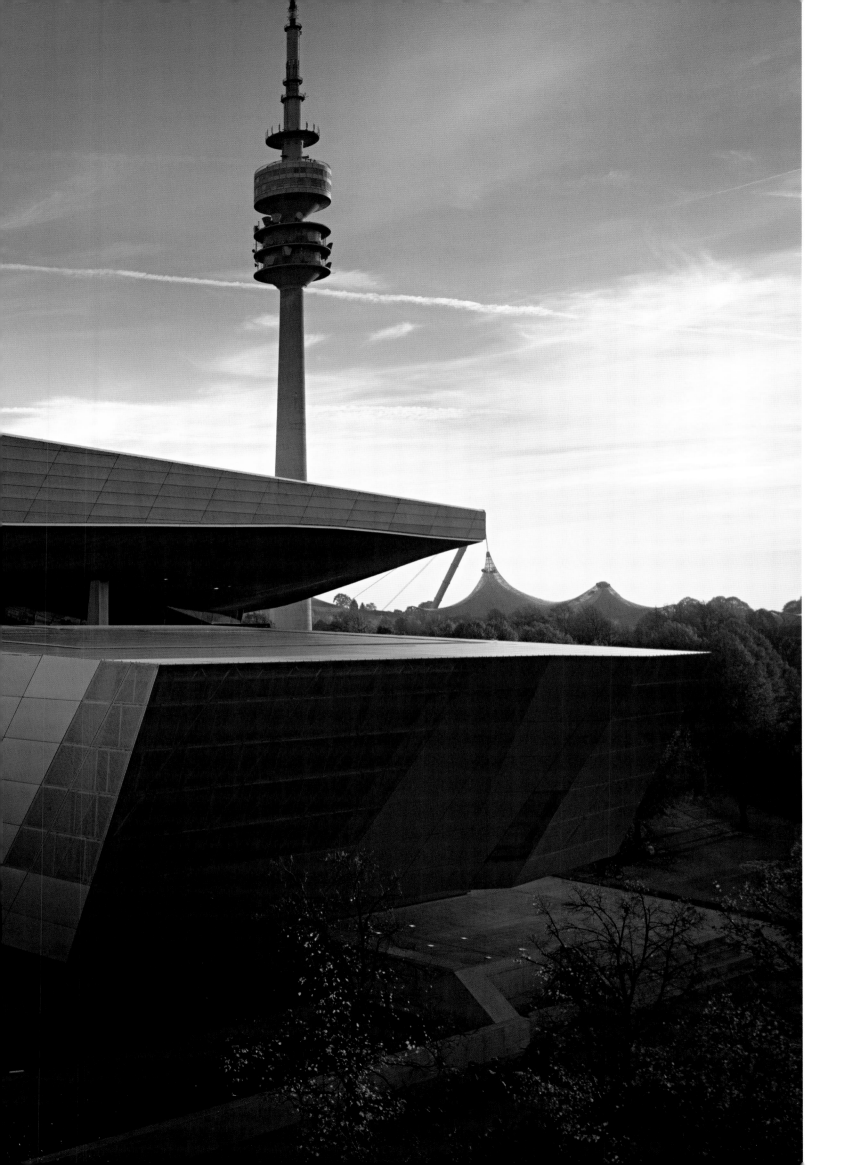

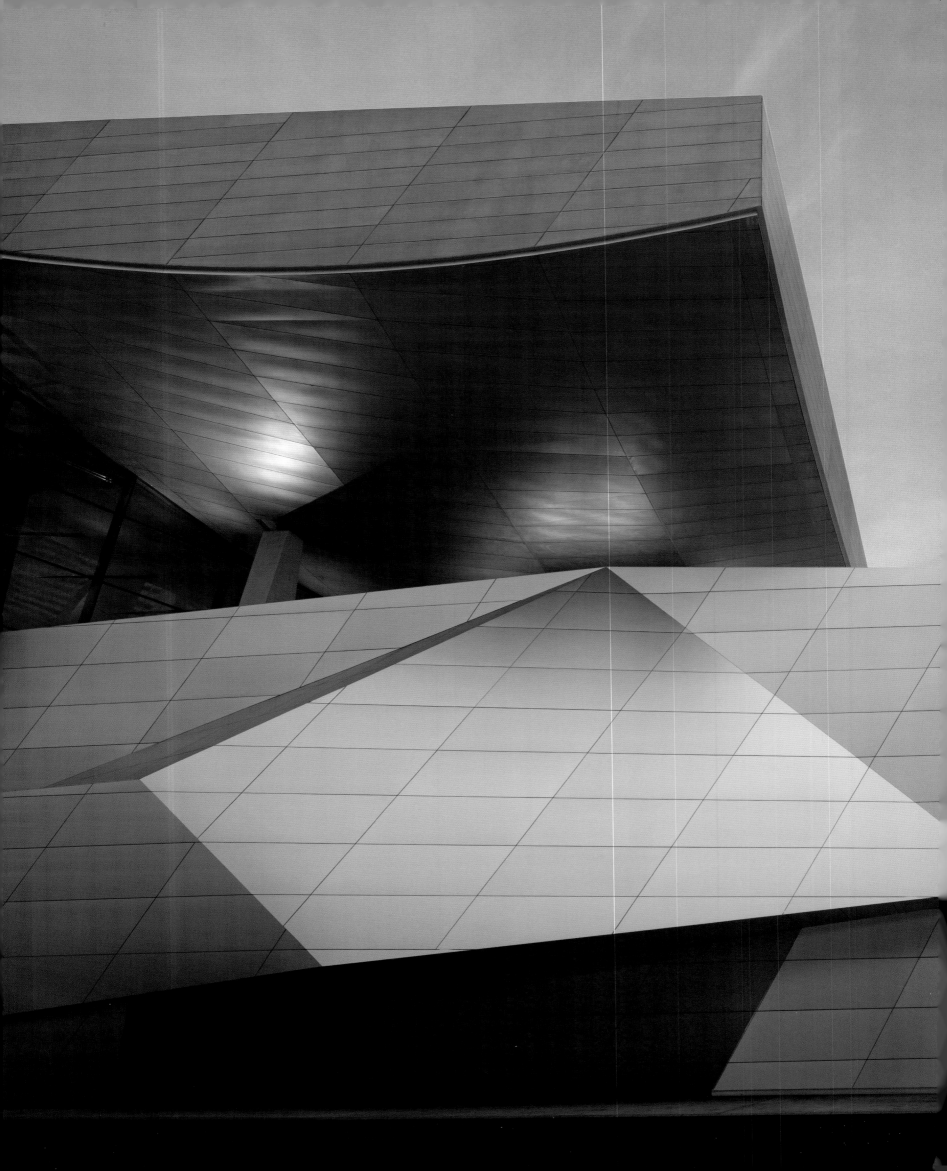

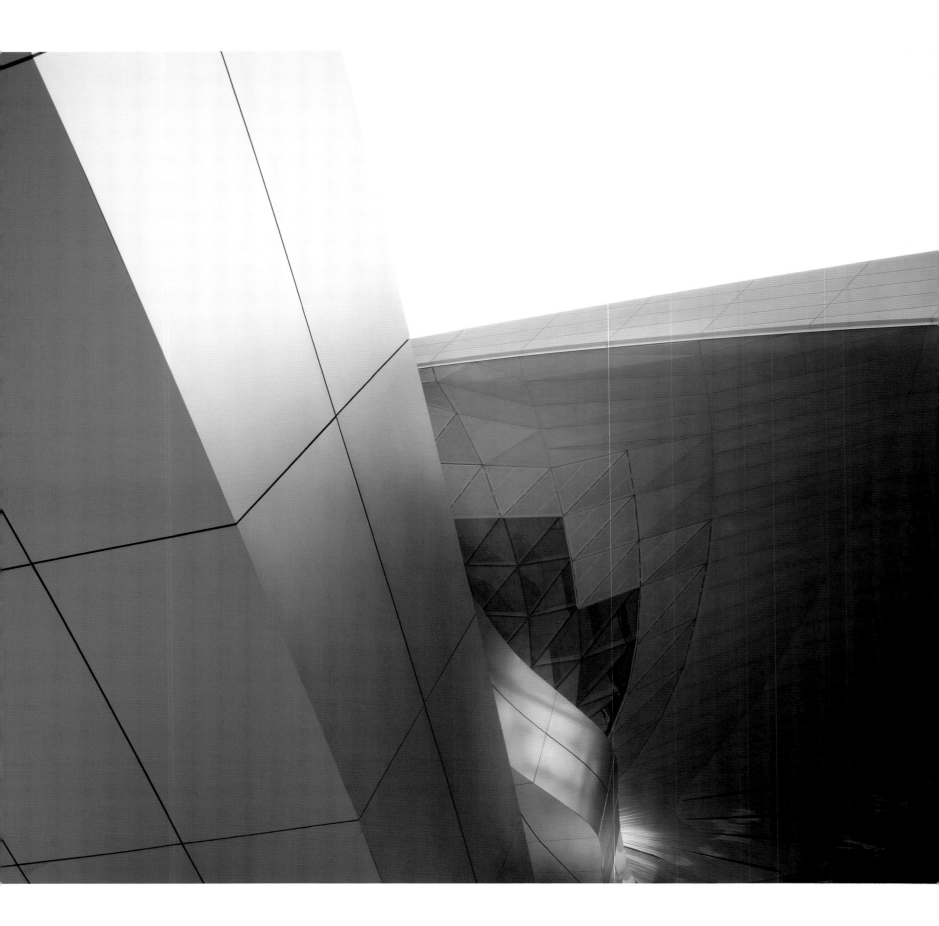

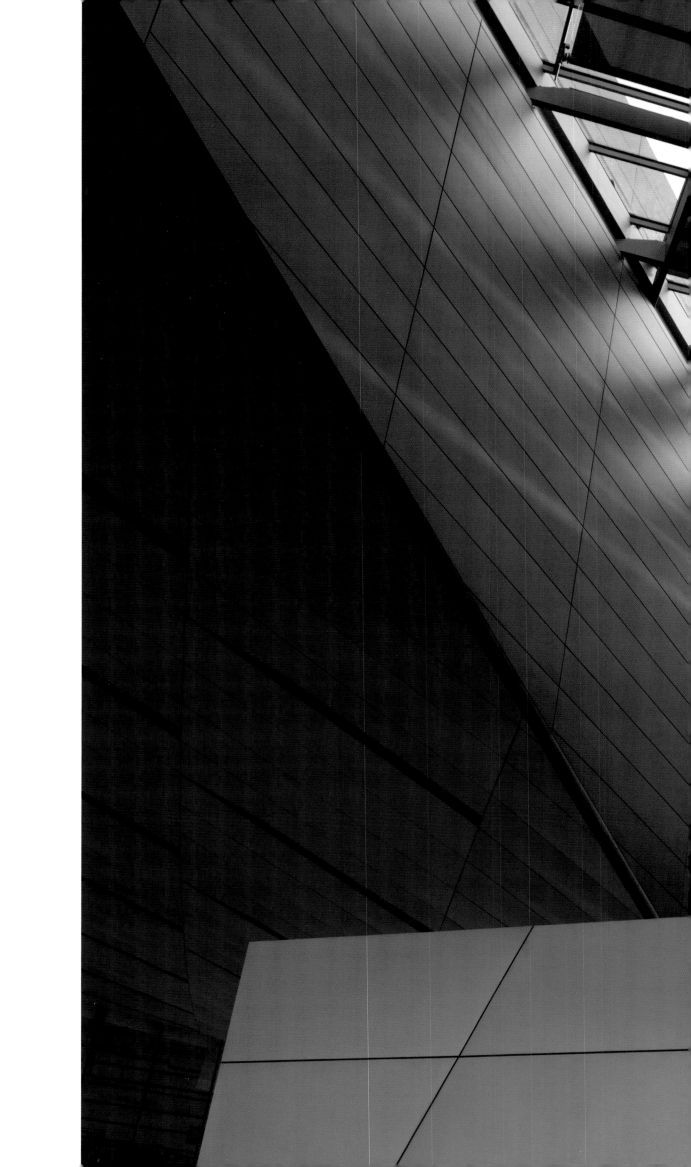

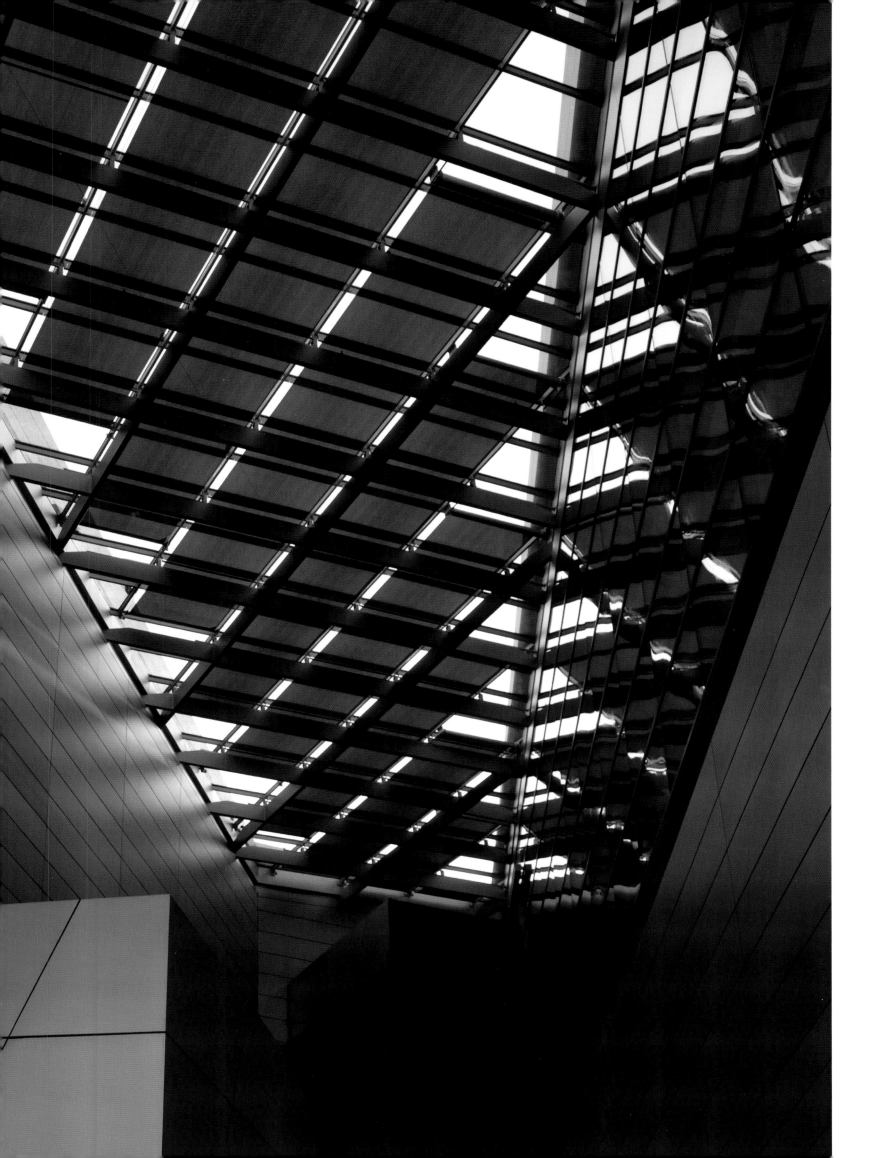

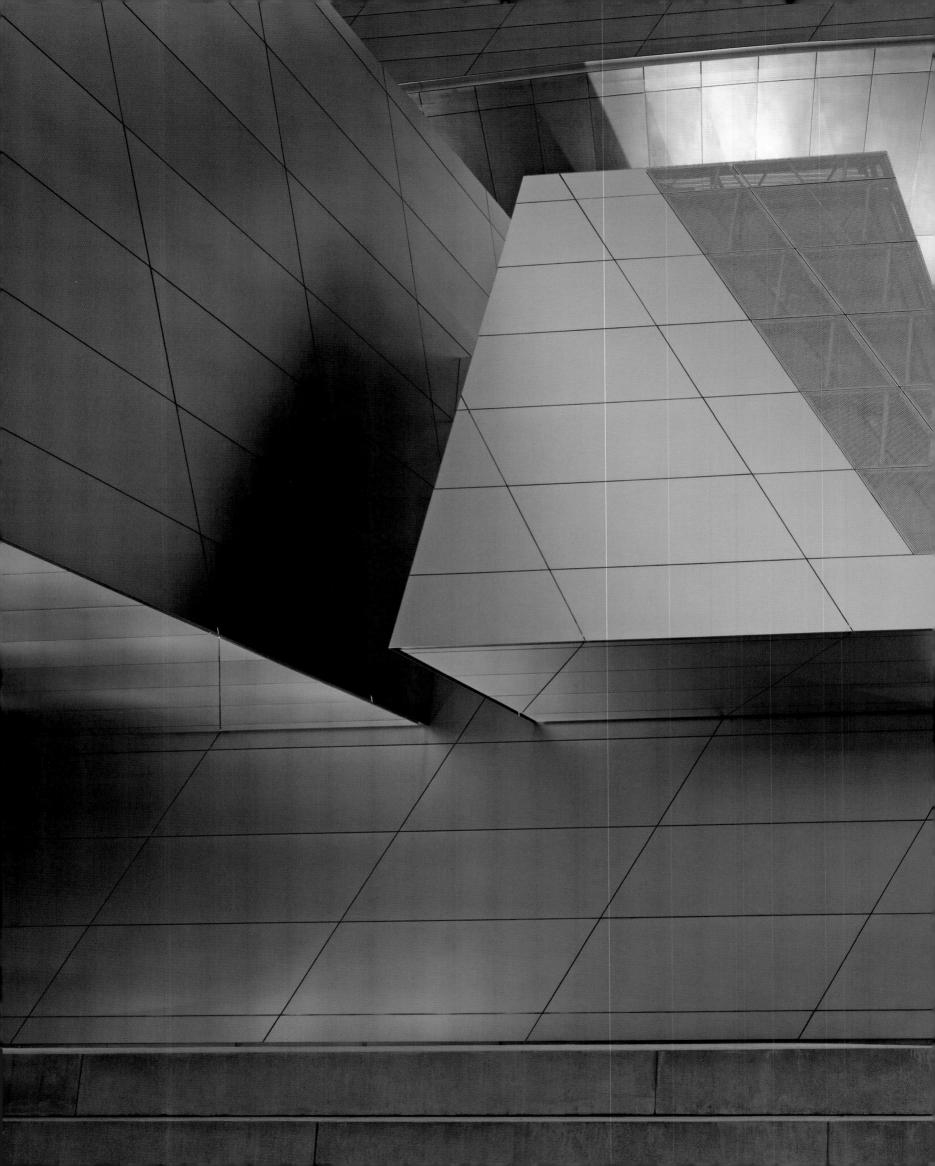

premiere _ premiere

Die Premiere ist das glanzvolle Herzstück der BMW Welt. Hier wird die Automobilauslieferung eindrucksvoll in Szene gesetzt. Im Kundenzentrum bekommt der Abholer nach ereignisreichen Stunden seinen Fahrzeugschlüssel persönlich überreicht und erlebt die Freude am Fahren auf ganz besondere Weise. Von hier aus unternimmt er die erste Fahrt in seinem neuen BMW. Für diesen emotionalen Moment kommen Kunden aus aller Welt nach München. Bis zu 250 Fahrzeuge können pro Tag übergeben werden. Oder anders formuliert: Alle zwei bis drei Minuten rollt ein Kunde mit seinem neuen Automobil hinaus in die Welt.

The Premiere is the glamorous centrepiece of the BMW Welt. Automobile delivery is staged and presented here in an impressive way. Following eventful hours in the customer centre, the customer is personally presented with his car keys and experiences sheer driving pleasure in a very special way. From here he begins his first drive in his new BMW. Customers come to Munich from all around the world for this emotional moment. Up to 250 vehicles can be handed over daily, or in other words: a customer drives out into the world in his new automobile every two to three minutes.

Das individuelle Erlebnis der Automobilauslieferung beginnt für den Kunden bereits bei seinem BMW Händler oder in der Niederlassung. Mit einem Vorlauf von mehreren Monaten kann er seinen Wunschtermin exakt bestimmen. Mit der Auftragsbestätigung für das Fahrzeug werden der konkrete Abholtag und der genaue Zeitpunkt der Übergabe festgelegt. Auftakt für den großen Tag in der BMW Welt ist die Anmeldung am Check In. Von diesem Zeitpunkt an übernehmen BMW Welt Mitarbeiter die Tagesplanung für den Kunden und veranlassen alles Weitere für den Augenblick der Automobilübergabe. Die individuelle Betreuung und Planung des Tagesprogramms steht hierbei im Vordergrund, um den Wünschen der Abholer optimal zu entsprechen. Auf einem Ticket werden alle wichtigen Daten wie zum Beispiel Führungen oder Zugangsberechtigungen vermerkt. Sie weisen dem Kunden an diesem Tag den Weg. In der Premium Lounge stehen Monitore bereit, die über den persönlichen Zeitpunkt der Automobilübergabe informieren. Hier unter dem Wolkendach der BMW Welt befindet sich exklusiv der Bereich für Kunden, die in Kürze ihren neuen BMW in Empfang nehmen. Die Betriebsamkeit der BMW Welt steht in auffallendem Gegensatz zur erwartungsfrohen Ruhe der Lounge, in der die zukünftigen Besitzer gespannt der Automobilübergabe entgegensehen. Vor dem großen Augenblick begleitet der Betreuer seinen Kunden jedoch zunächst in das Produkt Info Center. Während des Automobil-Briefings erfährt der Kunde hier alles über die technischen Besonderheiten und spannenden Details seines neuen BMW. Multimedial ausgestattete Themenstationen demonstrieren die Produkteigenschaften und bieten die Gelegenheit, sich mit der innovativen Technologie des Fahrzeuges auseinanderzusetzen. Wie leuchtet ein Scheinwerfer in die Kurve hinein, wenn man das Lenkrad bewegt? Was macht ein common rail mit Dieselkraftstoff? Wie arbeitet der BMW xDrive? Was versteht man unter BMW EfficientDynamics? Diese und viele andere Fragen werden hier gestellt und beantwortet. Die Kundenbetreuer gehen dabei individuell auf die Bedürfnisse des Abholers sowie auf die Ausstattung des bestellten Modells ein. Erste Station im Produkt Info Center ist der Info-Tisch. Hier geht es um Design, Performance, Service und Sicherheit. Auf Bildschirmen mit touchsensitiver Oberfläche erlebt der Kunde seinen persönlichen neuen BMW zum ersten Mal in Form von 3D Online Renderings. Bis zum individuellen Kennzeichen stimmt jedes Detail. Alle Themen, die am Info-Tisch angesprochen und gezeigt werden, sind auf das Modell abgestimmt. Nur für den Kunden relevante Informationen werden aufbereitet. Anschließend folgt die Einweisung am Info-Modul. Hier können Bedienkomfort und Fahrdynamik erprobt werden. Mit Hilfe eines Lenkrads, zweier Pedale und des iDrive Controllers lernt der Kunde die Eigenschaften seines BMW während einer virtuellen Probefahrt kennen. Für das sensorische Empfinden im Fahrzeug steht im Produkt Info Center das Wertigkeitsexponat zur Verfügung. Verschiedene Ledermuster beispielsweise verführen hier zum haptischen Begreifen und der Klang einer BMW Autotür wird zum akustischen Erlebnis.

Nach dem Automobil-Briefing und einem erneuten, kurzen Aufenthalt in der Premium Lounge steht der BMW auf der Premiere bereit. Wenn der Kundenbetreuer das Zeichen erhält, tritt der Kunde über die großzügige Galerietreppe den Weg zu seinem neuen Fahrzeug an. Zum exakt richtigen Zeitpunkt hat ein gläserner Aufzug das Automobil aus dem Tagesspeicher der BMW Welt auf die Premiere transportiert. Dort erwartet es auf einem

The individual experience of the automobile delivery already begins for the customer at his BMW dealer or in the branch. By placing an order some months in advance, the customer can exactly determine the desired date for collection. With the confirmation of the order for the vehicle, the precise day of collection and the exact moment of delivery are then confirmed. The beginning of the great day in the BMW Welt is the registration at the Check In desk. From this moment on, BMW Welt's personal assistants take over the day's timing schedule for the customer and initiate all that which is necessary for the moment when the automobile is handed over. The individual supervision and planning of the day's programme thus receives most emphasis, in order to optimally respond to the wishes of the customer. All the important particulars of the day are stored in the customer's ticket, such as guided tours or access authorization, and they show the customer his way around throughout the day. In the Premium Lounge, monitors are available to provide frequently updated information on the moment of the individual automobile hand-over. Here, beneath the cloud roof of the BMW Welt, the area exclusively for customers is to be found, who will shortly be receiving their new BMWs. The frenzy of activity in the BMW Welt stands in obvious contrast to the optimistic calmness of the lounge in which future owners excitedly look forward to their automobile delivery. Before the great moment however, the customer assistant firstly accompanies his customers into the Product Info Center. During the automobile briefing the customer learns all about the special technical features and exciting details of his new BMW. Multimedia-equipped info-points for various topics demonstrate product features and offer customers the chance to become acquainted with the innovative technology of the vehicle. How do the headlights shine into the bend in the road when one moves the steering wheel? What does a common rail do to diesel fuel? How does the BMW xDrive work? What does the company mean by BMW EfficientDynamics? These and many other questions are asked here and they are also answered. In so doing, the customer assistants cater to the individual requirements of the customer as well as to the optional equipment for the model that has been ordered. The first stop in the Product Info Center is the Info Table. The subject matter here is design, performance, service and safety. On monitors with touch-sensitive screens, the customer experiences his personalised, new BMW for the first time in the form of 3D online renderings. Every detail is perfectly presented, right up to the already specified licence plate. All topics that are approached and demonstrated at the Info Table are coordinated to the model in question, and only information relevant to the customer is dealt with. There then follows familiarisation at the Info Module, where handling comfort and driving dynamics can be tried out. With the aid of a steering wheel, two pedals and an iDrive controller the customer has the chance to get familiar with the characteristics of his BMW during a multi-media "test drive". The quality rating exhibit is available in the Product Info Center for the appraisal of sensorial impressions in the vehicle. Various leather samples for instance, beguile and tempt haptic appreciation, and the sound of a BMW car door becomes an acoustic experience.

Following the automobile briefing and a further short visit to the Premium Lounge, the new BMW is ready to be received on the Premiere. When the assistant receives the signal, the customer walks along the way to his new vehicle via the lavish gallery stairs. At precisely the right moment, a glass elevator transports the automobile

der 20 Drehteller oder einem der zehn Panoramaplätze seinen Besitzer. Die Inszenierung ist perfekt. Auf Hochglanz poliert und im Scheinwerferlicht funkelnd präsentiert sich der Höhepunkt des Tages – der neue BMW. Der unvergessliche Moment der ersten Begegnung ist da. Fahrzeugträume werden Wirklichkeit. Auf Wunsch des Kunden steht ein Fotograf bereit, der diesen Moment dokumentiert. Wenn die Scheinwerfer erlöschen und der Drehteller stoppt, steht das Fahrzeug so, dass der Abholer die Premiere problemlos über die Abfahrt verlassen kann. Kein unbequemes Rangieren, kein verlegenes Suchen nach dem richtigen Gang. Auch das mitgebrachte Gepäck wird vom Bellboy rechtzeitig zugeladen. Das Abholerfoto, ein Gruß des Händlers und ein Schlüsselanhänger mit persönlicher Gravur werden als Geschenk übergeben. Eine letzte, individuelle Einweisung durch den Betreuer, das Überreichen der Fahrzeugschlüssel und mit den ersten selbst gefahrenen Metern ist die Automobilauslieferung komplett. Die einmalige Atmosphäre der BMW Welt und der Blick auf die eindrucksvolle Architektur während des Hinausfahrens machen den Tag in der BMW Welt zu einem unvergesslichen Erlebnis.

from the BMW Welt's car storage up into the Premiere, and its new owner awaits it here at one of the 20 turn-tables or at one of the ten panorama spaces: The staging of the moment is perfect. With a brightly polished finish and under the glistening beam of the spotlights, the highlight of the day is presented – the new BMW, and the unforgettable moment of the first encounter has arrived. Automotive dreams come true. If desired by the customer, a photographer is standing by to record this special moment. When the spotlights are switched off and the turntable stops, the vehicle is so positioned that the customer can easily leave the Premiere via the exit ramp. No uncomfortable manoeuvring, no awkward searching for the right gearshift, even the luggage the customer brought with him is punctually loaded into the car by the bellboy. The delivery photograph, the dealer's greetings and a key-ring pendant with a personalized engraving are presented as a gift. A final, individual briefing by the assistant, the handing over of the vehicle's keys, and with the first few metres of driving by the new owner himself, automobile delivery is now completed. The unique atmosphere of the BMW Welt and the sight of the impressive architecture while driving off make the day spent here an unforgettable experience.

→ *Hubertus Hamm gehört zu den erfolgreichsten Fotografen Deutschlands. Für ihn ist Fotografieren eine Form der Begegnung, die eine offene Geste erfordert. Sein wichtigstes Anliegen in seiner fotografischen Auseinandersetzung ist die Unvoreingenommenheit, denn nur dadurch lassen sich distanzierte und objektivierende Wahrnehmungsmuster umgehen. Die spektakuläre Architektur der BMW Welt ist für Hubertus Hamm ein komplexer Ausdruck von Räumlichkeit, Perspektive, Konstruktion und Utopie – und damit deutlich mehr als nur ein Gebäude. Insofern ging es ihm bei seiner Arbeit nicht darum, den klassischen Blickwinkel eines Architekturfotografen einzunehmen. Er hat sich mit seiner Kamera dieser Architektur in einer Form der freien Konfrontation gestellt, abseits von Verallgemeinerung und sachlicher Darstellung. So entstanden Bilder, die interpretieren, und Bilder, die beim Betrachter möglicherweise neue Aspekte und Zusammenhänge aufzeigen. Seine Fotografien sind also auch ein Prozess der Kommunikation – eine lebendige Interaktion zwischen Fotograf und dem Objekt. Die Frage ist, wie seine Bilder dann die Wahrnehmung vor Ort und die Erinnerung an diesen Ort verändern. Und welche Vorstellung bei demjenigen erzeugt wird, der diese Architektur nur auf den Bildern sieht. Hubertus Hamm folgt beim Fotografieren seiner Inspiration und verlässt bewusst klassische Standpunkte. Er hat sich auf die Architektur der BMW Welt eingelassen und die Begegnung mit dem Objekt unbeeindruckt und entspannt gestaltet. Dadurch konnte Neues entstehen und das zu entdecken, ist die Einladung des Fotografen an den Betrachter.*

→ *Hubertus Hamm is one of Germany's most successful photographers. Photography is for him a form of encounter that requires an amenable gesture. His primary concern in his photographic exploration is the impartiality, since only in such a way can detached and objectifying patterns of perception be avoided. The spectacular architecture of the BMW Welt is for Hubertus Hamm a complex expression of spatiality, perspective, construction and utopia – significantly more than just a building. Therefore it was not a matter of him adopting the classical perspective of an architectural photographer for this project. With his camera he faced up to a form of free confrontation with this architecture, beyond all generalisation and objective presentation. Pictures thus emerged, which interpret, and others that perhaps reveal new aspects and correlations to the observer. His photographs are therefore also a process of communication – a living interaction between the photographer and the object. The question is, how do his pictures change the on-scene perception, and the recollection of this scene? And which impression does one receive if this architecture is seen only through the pictures? When photographing, Hubertus Hamm follows his inspiration and forsakes deliberately classical positions. He has become truly involved with the architecture of the BMW Welt and has nonchalantly and calmly sculpted the encounter with this structure. New facets thereby emerged, and the discovery of them is the invitation of the photographer to the beholder.*

meilensteine & technische daten _ timeline & technical information

11/01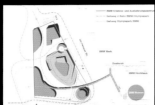

09/02

08/03

07/04

2001

► März *Der internationale Architekturwettbewerb wird ausgeschrieben. 275 Architekten reichen ihre Entwürfe ein.*

► Juli *Das Auswahlverfahren beginnt. Das Wiener Architekturbüro Coop Himmelb(l)au gewinnt gemeinsam mit dem Berliner Büro Sauerbruch Hutton den Wettbewerb.*

► November *BMW beantragt bei der Stadt München die Genehmigung für den Bau der BMW Welt.*

► Dezember *Der Vorstand der BMW AG entscheidet sich für die Realisierung des Entwurfs von Coop Himmelb(l)au.*

2002

► Januar *Die Bauphase beginnt mit statischen Berechnungen und ersten detaillierten Architekturskizzen.*

► September *Auf der Architektur-Biennale in Venedig wird der Öffentlichkeit erstmals ein Modell der BMW Welt präsentiert.*

2003

► Juli *Abschluss der Entwurfsplanung.*

► August *Baubeginn. Abbruch des Parkhauses West und der Park-and-Ride-Fläche.*

► November *Mit dem Aushub der Baugrube wird bereits begonnen.*

► Dezember *BMW reicht den Bauantrag ein.*

2004

► Januar *Die Pläne des Gebäudes liegen öffentlich aus. Der Spezialtiefbau beginnt.*

► Februar *Die Planung ist abgeschlossen. Die definitive Baugenehmigung wird bis zum Sommer erwartet.*

► Mai *In 14 Metern Tiefe ist die Talsohle der Baugrube erreicht. Insgesamt wurden 158.400 Kubikmeter Erdreich abtransportiert.*

► Juni *Der Rohbau der BMW Welt beginnt.*

► Juli *Zur feierlichen Grundsteinlegung der BMW Welt am 16. Juli sind 300 Gäste aus Politik, Wirtschaft und Kultur geladen.*

► August *Die Stadt München erteilt die verbindliche Baugenehmigung.*

► November *Auf der Ebene 0 werden die Fußpunkte für den Doppelkegel gesetzt. Der Stahlhochbau beginnt. Start der Stahlbau- und Fassadenarbeiten.*

2005

► Januar *Die Arbeit am Ausbau der Untergeschosse wird aufgenommen.*

► Februar *Der Rohbau der BMW Welt ist fertig.*

► Juli *Am 1. Juli ist Richtfest. Der höchste Punkt der Dachkonstruktion ist erreicht. Die Freigabe für den Innenausbau wird erteilt.*

► September *Mit dem Ausbau der Obergeschosse wird begonnen.*

► November *Nachdem das 16.000 m² große Dach eingedeckt ist, werden die Fotovoltaikelemente montiert.*

2006

► Juni *Die Untergeschosse der BMW Welt sind baulich fertig gestellt. Von einem Luftschiff aus verfolgen Sportjournalisten die Baufortschritte der BMW Welt.*

► Juli *Die Fassaden des Gebäudes sind geschlossen. Der Innenausbau des Business Center im Veranstaltungsforum beginnt.*

► November *Die Halle ist baulich abgeschlossen. Auch hier erfolgt jetzt der Innenausbau.*

► Dezember *Inbetriebnahme der Fotovoltaikanlage. Der erste operative Clustertest findet statt: Die Fahrzeugeinbringung ins Untergeschoss des Doppelkegels.*

2007

► Januar *Die Brücke zwischen der BMW Welt und dem BMW Museum ist fertig gestellt.*

► Februar *Beginn der Planung für den Innenausbau der Restaurants.*

► Mai *Kleiner Integrationstest. Funktionale Inbetriebnahme des Produkt Info Center.*

► Juni *Abschließender Integrationstest und Belastungstest. Bauübergabe. Es wird mit dem Innenausbau der Shops begonnen.*

► Juli *Erste Auslieferung an Pilotkunden (intern). Die BMW Welt bekommt ihre neue Adresse: Am Olympiapark 1. Der erste Gast wird in der Premium Lounge bewirtet. Der erste Küchenbereich (Premium Lounge) nimmt seinen Betrieb auf. Die Parkgeschosse werden fertig gestellt.*

► August *Die Lagerbereiche sind fertig gestellt und werden bezogen. Die Funktionalität wird getestet.*

► Oktober *Mitarbeiter der BMW Group bereiten die BMW Welt in einer Generalprobe am 4. Oktober für den Echtbetrieb vor. Am 17. Oktober wird die BMW Welt mit einem feierlichen Festakt eröffnet. Für die Öffentlichkeit ist das Erlebnis- und Auslieferungszentrum ab dem 20. Oktober zugänglich. Die ersten offiziellen Kunden holen ihr neues Automobil am 23. Oktober in der BMW Welt ab.*

02/05  06/06  07/07  10/07

2001

➤ **March** *March The international architectural competition calls for proposals. 275 architects submit their concepts.*

➤ **July** *The selection process begins. The Viennese architecture firm Coop Himmelb(l)au wins the competition jointly with the Berlin bureau of Sauerbruch Hutton.*

➤ **November** *BMW submits the BMW Welt scheme for approval by the City of Munich.*

➤ **December** *The BMW AG executive committee decides in favour of realising the Coop Himmelb(l)au concept.*

2002

➤ **January** *The construction phase begins with static calculations and the first detailed architectural sketches.*

➤ **September** *A model of the BMW Welt is presented in public for the first time at the International Architecture Biennale in Venice.*

2003

➤ **July** *Completion of outline planning.*

➤ **August** *Beginning of construction. Demolition of the Olympia parking block West and of the Park-and-Ride area.*

➤ **November** *Excavation work for the construction pit has already begun.*

➤ **December** *BMW submits building application.*

2004

➤ **January** *The building's plans are put on display in public. Special foundation construction begins.*

➤ **February** *Planning is finalised. The definitive building licence is expected by the summer.*

➤ **May** *At a depth of 14 metres the bottom level of the construction pit is reached. A total of 158,400 cubic metres of soil are removed from the site.*

➤ **June** *Construction of the BMW Welt building's shell begins.*

➤ **July** *At the BMW Welt's festive foundation-stone laying on 16th July, 300 guests are invited from political, economic and cultural circles.*

➤ **August** *The City of Munich issues the official building licence.*

➤ **November** *On level 0 the footings for the Double Cone are set in position. Construction of the steel shell begins. Start of structural steelwork and facade erection.*

2005

➤ **January** *Fitting out work on the underground levels begins.*

➤ **February** *Construction work on the BMW Welt shell is complete.*

➤ **July** *On 1st July the topping out ceremony takes place. The highest point of the roof construction is reached. Authorisation of interior construction is given.*

➤ **September** *Construction of the upper levels has begun.*

➤ **November** *Once the 16,000m² roof area is covered over, the photovoltaic units are mounted.*

2006

➤ **June** *The underground levels of the BMW Welt are structurally complete. Sport journalists follow construction progress of the BMW Welt from aboard a Zeppelin.*

➤ **July** *Facade surfaces of the building are completed. Interior construction of the Business Center in the Event Forum begins.*

➤ **November** *The main hall is structurally complete. Interior construction begins here too.*

➤ **December** *Commissioning of the photovoltaic installation. The first operative cluster test takes place: Introduction of vehicles into the underground level of the Double Cone.*

2007

➤ **January** *The bridge between the BMW Welt and the BMW Museum is completed.*

➤ **February** *Interior construction planning of the restaurants commences.*

➤ **May** *Minor integration test. Functional commissioning of the Product Info Center.*

➤ **June** *Conclusive integration test and test under load conditions. Building hand-over. Interior construction of the shops begins.*

➤ **July** *First vehicle deliveries to pilot customers (internal). The BMW Welt receives its new address: Am Olympiapark 1. The first guest is served in the Premium Lounge. The first kitchen area (Premium Lounge) goes into service. The parking levels are completed.*

➤ **August** *The car storage areas are completed and are occupied. Functionality is tested.*

➤ **October** *BMW Group personnel prepare the BMW Welt for real operations with a final rehearsal on 4th October. On 17th October the BMW Welt is opened with a festive ceremony. For the general public, the event and delivery centre is accessible from 20th October. The first official customers collect their new automobiles on 23rd October in the BMW Welt.*

Gebäude 180 m lang – nur wenig kürzer als ein ICE 3. 130 m breit. 28 m hoch – das entspricht etwa der Höhe der Bavaria auf der Theresienwiese mit Steinsockel. 7 Geschosse, davon 3 ober- und 4 unterirdisch. Ca. 25.000 m² Grundstücksfläche (etwa 3 Fußballfelder). Ca. 73.000 m² Bruttogeschossfläche Gesamt (etwa 10 Fußballfelder). 45.000 m² Untergeschossfläche. 28.000 m² oberirdische Geschossfläche. 531.000 m³ fasst das Gebäude. **Planungsphase** 120 Architekten und Ingenieure in der Ausführung, sowie 30 Subplaner. 800.000 Stunden dauerte die Planung. 25.000 ausgearbeitete Pläne in der Größe DIN A0, entspricht 2 Tonnen Papier. **Rohbau** 15.000 m² Baugrube, 210 m lang und 120 m breit. 158.400 m³ Aushub Baugrube (entspricht ca. 12.000 LKW-Ladungen). 775 Bohrpfähle (17 m tief, Ø 88 cm) bilden den wasserdichten Verbau. 14 m tief lag die Grubensohle (8 m unter Grundwasserspiegel). 3.6 Millionen m Stabstähle wurden verarbeitet – das entspricht fast einem Viertel des Erddurchmessers. 60.000 m³ Beton wurden insgesamt gegossen, 20.000 m³ alleine für die Bodenplatte. 10.000 t Betonstahl wurden eingebaut, 14.500 m² Glas und 10.000 m² Edelstahl wurden bei der Fertigstellung der Fassade montiert. Bis zu 800 Menschen arbeiteten gleichzeitig auf der Baustelle. **Dachkonstruktion** 16.000 m² Dachfläche (so groß wie der Markusplatz in Venedig). 4.000 t Stahl stecken in der Dachkonstruktion. 26 Rüsttürme stützten während der Bauphase das Dach, jetzt stemmen nur noch 11 filigrane Stützen und der Doppelkegel diese Masse. Das Dach wurde mit Hydraulikpressen gehoben und schließlich auf die 11 Stützen des Gebäudes selbst abgelastet. Min. 8 cm kann sich das Dach bei Temperaturschwankung bewegen. Diese Bewegungen werden am Dachrand u. a. durch einen Knick in der Fassade aufgenommen. Dieser wirkt wie eine Feder. Auf diese Weise können Bewegungsfugen etc. entfallen. 6.300 m² Fotovoltaikelemente (3.660 Module) mit einer Leistung von ca. 810 MWh pro Jahr. **Innenausbau** ca. 15.000 Leuchten im gesamten Gebäude. 2.700 kW Kühlleistung. 3.800 kW Wärmeleistung. 400.000 m³ bewegte Luft im Betrieb. 10.000 Sprinklerköpfe zum Löschen eventuell auftretender Feuer. 1.200 Türen führen in 1.154 Räume. 120 m lang ist die „Flaniermeile" in der Plaza. 4 Gastronomieeinheiten (Coffee Bar < Bistro < Restaurant International < Club Restaurant). 50 Sitzplätze Club Restaurant, 3. OG. 160 Sitzplätze Restaurant International, 2. OG. 150 Sitzplätze auf der Außenterrasse des Restaurant International. 80 Sitzplätze Bistro, EG. 20 Sitzplätze Coffee Bar, 2. OG. 700 m² BMW Shop mit Lifestyle- und Merchandising-Artikeln. 80 Minuten dauert die BMW Welt Tour Kompakt oder die BMW Welt Tour Architektur. Die Hälfte der Zeit benötigt die BMW Welt Tour Spezial (40 Minuten). **Inbetriebnahme** 584 Parkplätze. Ca. 200 neue Arbeitsplätze. Max. 284 Automobile warten im Tagesspeicher auf die Übergabe. 3.000 m² groß ist die Premiere, auf der Ø 170 (max. 250) Automobilauslieferungen pro Tag stattfinden. Ca. 45.000 Abholer pro Jahr, mit Begleitpersonen ca. 95.000. Ca. 850.000 Besucher jährlich. **Doppelkegel** 28 m Höhe (BMW Museum 25 m, BMW Hochhaus 104,5 m). 45 m Durchmesser. In 14 m Höhe Taillenknick. 720 t Gewicht beträgt die Gesamtkonstruktion.

Building 180m long – just shorter than a German ICE 3 train. 130m wide. 28m high – about equal to Munich's 'Bavaria' statue on the Theresienwiese, including the stone plinth. 7 levels, 3 of which are above ground and 4 underground. Ca. 25,000m² plot of land (ca. 3 football pitches). Ca. 73,000m² gross total floor area (ca. 10 football pitches). 45,000m² underground floor area. 28,000m² upper floors. 531,000m³ total building volume. **Planning phase** 120 architects and engineers in implementation, also 30 assistant planners. 800,000 hours spent in planning. 25,000 elaborated plans in size DIN A0, equals 2 tonnes of paper. **Shell of building** 15,000m² construction pit, 210m long and 120m wide. 158,400m³ excavated soil (equals ca. 12,000 truckloads). 775 bored piles (17m deep, Ø 88cm) form the waterproof retaining walls. 14m deep pit-bottom (8m below groundwater level). 3.6 million m of reinforcing rods were fabricated – equals almost a quarter of Earth's diameter. 60,000m³ concrete were poured in total, 20,000m³ for the raft foundation alone. 10,000t concrete reinforcing rods were used, 14,500m² glass and 10,000m² stainless steel were fitted for completion of the facade. Up to 800 people worked at any given time on the building site. **Roof construction** 16,000m² roof area (as big as St. Mark's Square in Venice). 4,000t steel used in roof construction. 26 scaffold towers supported the roof during construction, now only 11 slender supports and the Double Cone hold up this weight. The roof was lifted by hydraulic jacks and finally lowered onto 11 supports of the building itself. The roof can easily move about 8cm due to temperature fluctuation. These movements are absorbed at the roof's edge via a kink in the facade which functions like a spring. Thus expansion joints etc. are avoided. 6,300m² photovoltaic units (3,660 modules) with a capacity of ca. 810MWh annually. **Interior fittings** ca. 15,000 lights in the entire building. 2,700kW cooling capacity. 3,800kW heating capacity. 400,000m³ circulated air during working hours. 10,000 sprinkler heads as extinguishers in case of fire. 1,200 doors lead into 1,154 rooms. 120m long is the 'promenade' in the Plaza. 4 gastronomic units (Coffee Bar < Bistro < Restaurant International < Club Restaurant). 50 seating places in Club Restaurant, 3rd level. 160 seating places in Restaurant International, 2nd level. 150 seating places on the terrace of Restaurant International. 80 seating places in Bistro, ground floor. 20 seating places in Coffee Bar, 2nd level. 700m² BMW Shop with lifestyle and merchandising articles. 80 minutes is spent on BMW Welt Tour 'Compact' or BMW Welt Tour 'Architecture'. The BMW Welt Special Tour takes half the time (40 minutes). **Commissioning** 584 parking spaces. Ca. 200 new jobs. Max. 284 automobiles wait in car storage for their hand-over. 3,000m² is the Premiere's extent, in which on average 170 (max. 250) automobile deliveries take place daily. Ca. 45,000 customers collect their new cars annually, with companions ca. 95,000 persons. Ca. 850,000 visitors annually. **Double Cone** 28m high (BMW Museum: 25m, BMW Tower: 104.5m). 45m diameter. Its waist kink is 14m high. 720t is the total weight of its construction.

ABO Glasreinigungs GmbH: Agnes Mierzer **ag Licht:** Klaus Adolph, Birgit Bierbaum, Yvonne Goldschmidtböing, Cieh-Chieh Hwang, Wilfried Kramb, Michaela Kruse, Clifton Pinathi, Daniel Walden **Allround Service:** Monica Nadal **Alphabet (BMW Group):** Karl-Heinz Kral **ALSCO Berufskleidung-Service GmbH:** Robert Wildgruber, Michael Zywietz **Appel Fördertechnik GmbH:** Thomas Appel, Michael Berg, Michael Hirschböck, Wolfgang Papenforth, Boris Smid **aquadetox international:** Klaus Buck, Heidrum Halder, Sybilla Heller, Anatol Jung, Hans Jörg Kohler, Roland Lorch, Margarete Münsch, Jürgen Schaible, Markus Schatz, Gabriella Schmid, Sebastian Schubert, Waltraut Weber **Architekturbüro Gotthard Seitz:** Gotthard Seitz **Architekturbüro Wagner:** Christoph Wagner **Argonauten 360:** Björn F. Christensen, Angela Mayer, Mathias Sinn **Aromata International:** Beate Nagel, Kurt L. Nübling, Thomas Socher **ART+COM AG:** Katharina Vollus, Andreas Wiek, Hans-Jörg Woite **Arxes:** Thomas Fischer, Harald Rieder, Bernd Schönberner **Auer & Partner GmbH:** Harald Gross, Dr. Josef Hopfgartner **Aufbau GmbH:** Oliver Falck, Rene Knaak, Kummrow Lars, Peter Lieberhof, Andreas Mohaupt, Ricky Möller, Ralf Schmitt, Volker Schmitt **Augustin Fassadenplanungs GmbH:** Alois Augustin **Autobus Oberbayern:** Maja Fahlbusch **Autohaus Friedrich GmbH & Co. KG:** Barbara Friedrich **Autohaus Fulda:** Peter Enders **Autohaus Spaett GmbH:** Paul Spaett **Automag Buchner + Linse:** Cathrine Batdorf **Avantgarde Gesellschaft für Kommunikation mbH:** Alexander Böttcher, Frank Eichhorn, Guido Emmerich, Kerstin Lindhuber, Christoph Meyden, Martin Schnaak, Andreas Schreiner, Christine Zecherle **B+G Ingenieure:** Jürgen Aßmus, Alexander Berger, Klaus Bollinger, Kyra Denk, Katja Diehl, Heike Ebert, Simone Frey, Manfred Grohmann, Bernd Heidlindemann, Arne Hofmann, Walter Karst, Robert Krüger, Michaela Mayer, Daniel Pfanner, Jörg Schneider, Ulrike Simon, Richard Troelenberg, Michael Wagner, Matthias Witte, Ulrich Wuttke **Bardusch GmbH & Co. KG:** Constantin Axtmann, Andrea Eisele, Michael Trutter **Bäuerle Stahlbau GmbH:** Florian Bäuerle **Bayerische Landesarchitektenkammer:** Michael Klingseisen **Bayerischer Lehrer- und Lehrerinnenverband:** Dr. Albin Dannhäuser **Bayerisches Staatsministerium f. Wirtschaft:** Hermann Friedrich **BAYERN TOURISMUS Marketing GmbH:** Richard Adam, Katja Austen-Gravel, Holger Kenngott, Katrin Lenz, Claudia Mitchell, Dr. Martin Spantig **BBF:** Ulf Bonfert, Martina Defner, Wolfgang Fergen, Florian Müller **BCG:** Lars Fillmann, Florian Schepp **BCM:** Susanne Bischof **Bearing Point:** Marcus Clemente, Uwe Kriegshäuser, Frank Liening, Peter Niedermayer **BECC:** Leif Geuder, Mario Krueger **BEKRA Hydrokulturen Vertriebs-GMBH:** Erika Gronert, Jörg Gronert **BELA Gmbh:** Harald Orthofer, Robert Peters, Tobias Seidel **Bezirksausschuss:** Ingeborg Staudenmeyer, Antonie Thomsen **Bezirksausschuss 24 Feldmoching Hasenbergl:** Dr. Rainer Grossmann **bfm:** Benjamin Brunßen, Dieter Brunßen, Christian Buresch, Stephan Cordes, Christian Fritz, Andreas Geiss, Katrin Leykam, Christine Lindner, Marc-Olivier Stellwag **Blue Scope Communications Projektgesellschaft mbH:** Sylvia Demes, Sven Haas, Thomas Prahl, Uwe Prell, Christoph Schmuck, Mischa Schulze, Ivo Schuppe, Andreas Stephan **BMW Group:** Joachim Adamek, Michael Albrecht, Ruth Alfes-Kallenborn, Tom Allemeier, Elisabeth Allmaier, Kathrin von Alten, Joachim Altweck, Per Ankersen, Antonio Antela, Gertraud Antholzer, Carola Anwander, Christa Arius, Dieter Armannsberger, Dr. Wolfgang Armbrecht, Frank-Peter Arndt, Dr. Cosmas Asam, Hans Werner Baase, Dieter Bacher, Christian Bächer, Alexander Bachner, Michael Baer, Christopher Bangle, Uwe Bantzhaff, Michael Bartel, Karl Barzal, Andrea Bauer, Anna Bauer, Gerhard Bauer, Maria-Barbara Bauer, Martin Bauer, Petra Bauer, Ernst Baumann, Martina Baumann, Wolfgang Baumann, Karl Baumer, Christian Beck, Susanne Becker, Karl-Heinrich Beetz, Friedrich Behle, Dr. Gabriele Behrens, Christian Beier, Damir Berberovic, Horst Berger, Reimund Berger, Angela Berghahn, Harald Bertz, Klaus-Jürgen Berzl, Christine Beuthner-Keck, Helfried Binder, Andreas Binderberger, Dr. Joachim Bischof, Michael Blabst, Brian Blank, Roland Blechinger, Joachim Blickhäuser, Harald Block, Jürgen Böhler, Michael Bomann, Stefan Borbe, Fritz Bourauel, Dr. Thomas Brakensiek, Michael Bräkler, Christian Brandl, Dr. Andreas Braun, Manfred Bräunl, Christian Breit, Susanne Breitenberger, Oskar Brem, Uwe Brendel, Michaela Brenner, Anton Brenninger, Timm Brönner, Michael Bronsert, Matthias Brose, Wieland Bruch, Robert Brückl, Markus Bruger, Josef Brunner Ludwig Brunnmeier, Jürgen Brzank, Anette Buchta-Krell, Oliver Büchter, Hans-Joachim Bühlhoff, Stephan Bujnoch, Jan Burgemeister, Peter Burkardt, Rolf Burkhardt, Thomas Cannon, Sebastian Carl, Konstanze Carreras, Wilhelm Christian Cartsburg, Michael Caspers, Guy Chalmers, Michail Chiladakis, Sonja Chromek, Wolfgang Clemens, Ulrich Commer, Dr. Christian Cozzarini, Kerstin Dahnert, Ursula Daidrich, Ulrich Dangelmeyer, Anton Dankerl, Anke Dannerbeck, Martina Daschinger, Gerhard Daum, Kurt Degenhart, Matthias Detje, Helga Diebald, Danielle Dieben, Frank Diepen, Birgit Dierolf, Dr. Herbert Diess, Anna Elisabeth Dietinger, Bärbel Dietmann, Uwe Dietrich, Katja Dietz, Elisabeth Dirr, Peter Dirrigl, Ursula Distl, Michael Doerle, Josef Doerr, Julian Dommaschk, Ariane Dorner, Thomas Dorschner, Christiane Draeger, Dr.-Ing. Klaus Draeger, Uwe Drescher, Josef Drexler, Lindsay Duffield, Erwin Duschl, Reinhard Eberl, Bernd Eberle, Franz Edda, Jan Edelmann, Manfred Eder, Diane Edfelder, Josef Eggerstorfer, Dieter Ehlert, Stefan Eich, Friedrich Eichiner, Helmut Eichinger, Dr. Marc Eisenbarth, Manfred Eisenschmid, Gerald Eiser, Uwe Ellinghaus, Klaus-Richard Els, Karin Elvers, Jürgen Endres, Werner Entenmann, Thomas Eppel, Tobias Erfurth, Erhan Ergen, Carola Erlewein, Christine Ernst, Peter Ernst, Angelika Espinosa, Marcus Essenpreis, Gerd Faber, Eckhard Fahrentholz, Gabriele Faltermeier, Maria Felber, Vera-Adrienne Fellner, Thomas Fels, Dr. Rainer Feurer, Volker Figura, Alexander Fischer, Rainer Fischer, Angelika Fleischer, Stephan Fleischer, Horst Flinspach, Arndt Focken, Herbert Forster, Ernst Fortune, Anthony Foulk, Alexander Franke, Andre Franz, Dr. Harald Franze, Raymond Freymann, Jörg Friebel, Wolfgang Fried, Ellen Friedel, Dr. Oliver Friedmann, Ralf Fries, Renate Fritz-Reymann, Friedrich Fruth, Dr. Robert Füchsle, Andreas Fürst, Stefan Gabriel, Klaus Gärtner, Katrin Gagzow, Andreas Gambeck, Ulrich Gamel, Dr. Michael Ganal, Ramos García, Richard Gaul, Margit Gaydoul, Ferdinand Geckeler, Claudia Geipel, Joachim Geissler, Jens Gerhardt, Fritz Geri, Marco Gerleit von Eynatten, Karl H. Gerlinger, Richard Gerstner, Sabine Geserer, Yasmin Ghavami, Christine Gietl, Eduard Gietl, Thomas Giuliani, Nadine Giusti, Ralf Glenewinkel, Thomas Glub, Reinhard Göhler, Raimund Gorny, Prof. Dr. - Ing. E.h. Senator Burkhard Göschel, Tilmann Gottesleben, Christine Gowdridge, Gunther Grabbe, Russel Grady, Felix Graf, Markus Graf, Gabriele Grahammer, Grit Grassberger, Dr. Werner Grassl, Ina Grassmann, Dr. Herbert Grebenc, Michael Greiffenberg, Dr. Hans-Robert Greim, Uwe Greiner, Wolfram Greiner, Thomas Grenz, Christian Greve, Stephan Grimm, Marc Groenninger, Kai Grohmann, Karl-Heinz Grohmann, Marc Grönninger, Klaus-Jürgen Gross, Christoph Gross, Bernhard Grüber, Manfred Grunert, Herbert Grünsteidl, Sylvia Gschoederer, Oliver Gschwandtner, Pia Guerra-Müller, Monika Gürtler, Ulrike Hagel, Adrian von Hagemeister, Friederike Hähle, Peter Hahn, Thomas Hahn, Tobias Hahn, Gudrun Hain, Anton Haller, Barbara Hamberger, Tobias Hannig, Andrea Hanrieder, Sebastian Happ, Franz Harlander, Felix Hartl, Christoph Hartmann, Werner Hartwig, Nils Hasse, Ulla Hassler, Christian Haudeck, Hans Haumer, Lutz Haupt, Markus Häusel, Klaus Hauser, Bernhard Hausmaninger, Dr. Christian Hayler, Rainer Heid, Karlheinz Heilmann, Jörg Heine, Christian Heinmüller, Mark Heinrich, Dieter Helling, Daniela Helmer, Andreas Hemmerle, Ralf Henning, Joachim Hensel, Manuela Hermann, Robert Hermann, Thomas Herrmann, Michael Heuler, Ernst von Heyking, Claudia Hierath, Alexander Hildebrandt, Dieter Hilsch, Helmut Himmel, Ulrich Hirschle, Andreas Hocke, Denis Hocke, Dr. Janett Hoellmueller, Dr. Christoph Hoerster, Harald Hofbauer, Hans-Dieter Hoffbauer, Gerhard Hoffmann, Marlies Hoffmann, Rudolf Höfler, Thilo Hofmann, Dirk Hollweg, Martina Holtmann-Singer, Oliver Holz, Markus Hölzel, Manfred Holzer, Alois Hölzle, Maria Holzner, Roland Holzner, Georg Hopfenmüller, Stephan Horn, Christian Huber, Franz Huber, Ralph Huber, Jörg-Dieter Hübner, Rudolf Hudler, Dr. Alexander Huesmann, Eckhard Hujer, Christian Humele, Christoph Huss, Ralf Hussmann, Werner Hutter, Klaus Igl, Anna Ilg, Bernd Imhof, Franz Inzko, Frank Isenberg, Leon Jacobs, Alfred Jänicke, Erwin Jänker, Vera Jagenberg, Gerald Jagersbacher, Marco Janak, Andrea Janneck, Andre Janssen-Timmen, Michael Jetzig, Harald Juenke, Achim Juhl, Jeanette Jungwirth-Huber, Inga Jürgens, Viktor Kabath, Robert Kachel, Thomas Kachel, Michael Kachl, Michael Kaefer, Andreas Kaffka, Tobias Kagerer, Corinna Kaiser, Sinja Kaiser, Thomas Kaiser, Max Kalbfell, Anja Kalchschmid, Axel Kaltwasser, Daniel Kammerer, Drazena Kantarevic, Kathrin Kapser, Stefan Karch, Saladin Karl, Kai Karsten, Stafan Keck, Dr. Timm Kehler, Henning Kelch, Dr. Bernhard Keller, Bernhard Kellerer, Günther Kellerer, Markus Kemper, Karl Kern, Holger Kersten, Dirk Kessler, Dr. Hans-Peter Ketterl, Anna Kiefer, Susann Kiessling, Berthold Kilian, Andrew Kirby,

Barbara Kirchner, Hanno Kirner, Thomas Kirsch, Michael Kirsch, Simone Kister, Heinrich Kleist, Jenny Kley, Christian Klinger, Martin Klink, Alfred Klomfass-Boek, Christian Kloss, Monique Kluge, Uwe Knebelsberger, Norbert Knerr, Ulrich Knieps, Ina Knoblach, Joachim von Knobloch, Jutta Knoedl, Elisabeth Knör, Christian Knötzele, Jan-Christiaan Koenders, Christiane Koenitzer, Roland Kohler, Petra Köhrer, Martin Kolessa, Jürgen Korzer, Paul Kosin, Jürgen Köster, Joanna Kostrz, Anja Kottmeier, Jörg Kottmeier, Christian von Kotze, Franz-Xaver Kraft, Gerald Krainer, Michael Krammer, Ottmar Kratzer, Helmut Kraus, Stefan Krause, Peter Kreisbeck, Michael Kreitmeier, Alexander Kremer, Dirk Kretschmer, Jana Kreutzmann, Ansgar Kreuzer, Heinz Krusche, Thomas Kruse, Georg Kügler, Holger Kügler, Thorsten Kühnel, Martin Kulessa, Sonal Kumar, Thomas Kupsch, Dr. Hans-Michael Kurz, Nadine Kurz, Stephan Kürzinger, Astrid Kuwilsky, Oliver La Bonte, Felix-Hendrik Laabs, Ulrike Lange, Marcus Lanzl, Holger Lapp, Richard von Laszewski, Holger Lau, Herbert Laub, Silke Lazarus, Rudolf Lechelmayr, Gabriele Lechner, Doris Lehmann, Hubert Lehnert, Ernst Leidenberger, Thomas Leidenberger, Georg Leidinger, Margit Leiminger, Jens Lemon, Thomas Lenz, Ulrich Lenz, Bernhard Lenzen, Georg Lerner, Andreas Lev, Dirk Lewanzik, Thomas Lichtenberger, Melanie Lipp, Hans Lippert, Werner Löchel, Simone Lockert, Dieter Loechelt, Markus Löken, Doris Lönner, Simone Löprich, Silvia Lorenz, Gerold Löschan, Romy Lucke, Dr. Stefanie Ludorf-Ring, Simon Luijckx, Frank Lutter, Michael Lütticke, Stefan Lutz, Wilhelm Macholej, Michael Mägel, Silvia Maid, Birgit Maier, Tobias Maier, Johannes Maierhofer, Fritz Maiterth, Csaba Major, Harald Mall, Inge Mamani-Vasquez, Marco Mangini, Ines Mangold, Gewnael Marchadour, Ernst Marqutsch, Stefan Martin, Petra Marz, Martina Marzy, Nadine Mascarenhas, Steffen Maucher, Dr. Karl May, Bernd Mayer, Annette Mayerbacher, Dr. Paul Mayonga, Annett Meerboth, Bruno Mehler, Andreas Mehlhase, Ulrich Mehring, Alexandra Meigel, Alois Meindl, Christian Meindl, Thomas Meinhardt, Frank Meissner, Marcus Meister, Volker Melzer, Elisabeth von Mengden, Ina Menge, Harald Metz, Katja Meurer, Lothar Meyer, Peter Meyer, Marc Mielau, Gregor Miklik, Wilhelm Mikolajetz, Prof. Dr. - Ing. E.h. Senator Joachim Milberg, Stephan Milke, Franz Mirlach, Jutta Missios-Aigner, Nikolaos Mitritzikis, Jutta Moder, Jürgen Mohr-Herbst, Werner Möhrlein, Stefan Mokosch, Herbert Morbitzer, Stefan Morell, Miguel Morgado, Erich Moser, Wolfgang Moser, Alwin Mrotzek, Rostislav Muchitsch, Thomas Muderlak, Reinhard Muehlbauer, Robert Mueller, Torsten Mueller-Oetvoes, Angelika Müller, Beate Müller, Dr. Steffen Müller, Guido Müller, Jochen Müller, Robert Müller, Oliver Munder, Regina Nachtmann, Linhardt Naucke, Josef Nauderer, Udo Naumann, Alexander Necke, Christine Neckelmann, Bettina Neu, Björn Neumann, Markus Neumayer, Karin Neumeier, Max Neumeier, Martina Neuschäfer, Markus Newedel, Dr. Tobias Nickel, Gerhard Nieborowski, Friedrich Nitschke, Peter Nockmann, Tarek Nouri, Wolfgang Nowotny, Wolfgang Obermaier, Susanne Obermeier, Helmar Oehm, Axel Oesterling, Michael Olbrück, Fabio Olivotti, Nikola von Ondarza-Röhreke, Robert Oostendorp, Haluk Oran, Roderik von Ostrowski, Hendrik Otte, Ramazan Özdemir, Dr. Helmut Panke, David Panton, Maximilian Pasternak, Josefine Patzelt, Antje Pauli, Dr. Jürgen Pawlik, Klaus Pechtl, Andreas Penkin, Andreas Penz-kofer, Gerrit Peters, Ulrike Pfaffmann, Gunther Pfau, Hoang Hai Pham, Corinna Picker, Christoph Pietrek, Christian Pingitzer, Lisa Pirwitz, Karl Pirzer, Thomas Pittino, Anna Pletschacher, Lothar Pletz, Dunja Poelt, Gerhard Pohl, Jürgen Pohl, Patrick Pohland, Joachim Pöhlmann, Franz Poisel, Ivan Poklecki, Claus Polap, Gerhard Popp, Helmut Pöschl, Timo Poser, Holger Pothmann, Michael Pöttker, Manfred Pötzinger, Johannes Prantl, Carsten Pries, Erwin Primas, Erich Projer, Guenther Prokop, Fritz-Werner Proksch, Helmut Puchner, Jutta Quade, Dr. Ulrich Quay, Günther Raab, Falko Radomski, Klaus Radtke, Michael Rahe, Ralf Rahn, Wiebke Ramlon, Robert Ratay, Hans-Juergen Redder, Wolfgang Rehaber, Stephan Reiff, Jörg Reimann, Franz Reimer, Martin Reischl, Karl-Ulrich Reisenweber, Anton Reisinger, Dr. Josef Reiter, Dr.-Ing. Norbert Reithofer, Frank Reitz, Ibrahim Rhawi, Matthias Richter, Reiko Richter, Dr. Thomas Rinn, Dr. Ralf Rodepeter, Hans-Erdmann von Roedern, Carsten Röger, Joachim Rössler, Anne Rohstock, Thomas Roller, Christian Röpenack, Susanne Rosche, Dagmar Rose, Ariane Rosenfelder, Bernd Rosenlehner, Dr. David Ross, Bernhard Rossi, Mona Ruessmann, Manfred Rüggeberg, Markus Sagemann, Karl Saladin, Christian Salge, Johann Saller, Jennifer Salling, Alexander Säring, Andreas Sauer, Ekaterina Saven-kova, Rajiv Saxena, Laurenz Schaffer, Bernd Schaible, Oliver Schaich, Beate Schaller, Edith Schaller, Marco Scharfe, Natalie Scharl, Sibylle Scharrenberg, Gabriele Schat-tat, Rolf Scheibner, Wolfgang Scheidler, Karen Schellenberg, Jone Scherf, Klaus Scheuerer, Andreas Schiessler, Christian Schiffmann, Ernst Schindler, Dr. Armin Schirmer, Dirk Schirrmacher, Michael Schlammer, Angelika Schmid, Karl-Heinz Schmid, Wilhelm-Georg Schmid, Lothar Schmidle, Daniel Schmidt, Dr. Michael Schmidt, Stefan Schmidt, Thomas Schmidt, Gabi Schmitt, Dr. Georg Schmitz, Max Schneider, Simone Schneider, Nicole Schober, Maximilian Schöberl, Manfred Schoch, Christian Schoemezler, Otto Schoffer, Martin Schoper, Jürgen Schrag-Richter, Dr. Markus Schramm, Markus Schreier, Eberhard Schrempf, Gabriele Schreyer, Johann Schuberthan, Dr. Gerhard Schuff, Dr. Caroline Schulenburg, Christine Schult, Mike Schulz, Ulrich Schünemann, Carsten Schürenberg, Sabine Schürhoff-Dobler, Claudia Schütte, Rico Schütz, Hans Schweiger, Annette Schweizer, Carmen Schwindl, Jürgen Scupin, Thomas Seelbach, Christoph Seger, Kay Segler, Anja Seibert, Christine Seidel, Werner Seidel, Sandra Seitner, Ralph Seitz, Thomas Senser, Dr. Julia Sernetz, Thomas Sieber, Rolf Siegel, Hans-Reinhart Sigl, Volker Simon, Monika Sippel, Ian Skelton, Anita Skocic, Bernhard Sommer, Sabine Sowa, Robert Spaderna, Joachim Spangenberg, Reinhard Spelsberg, Horst Spickenreuther, Holger Spikermann, Florian Spinoly, Kurt Sposta, Johannes Spreng, Gerhard Springer, Jakob Stangl, Martin Starringer, Sabine Staschik, Benno Stechele, Alfred Steiner, Monika Steiner, Philipp Steinle, Dr. Eckhard Steinmeier, Dr. Georg Stellner, Elisabeth Stemmler, Nicole Stempinsky, Christian Stieglmaier, Rudolf Stingl, Oliver Stockhecke, Alexandra Stöckl, Götz-Rüdiger Stoll, Robert Stoller, Pierre Stommel, Christiane Straubinger, Martin Straubinger, Monika Strauch, Heike Strich, Martin Strobel, Eva Strohmeyer, Günter Stumfoll, Thomas Summerer, Ralf Sussani, Dr. Regine Sweens, Manfred Swoboda, Peter Szczeponik, Natascha Tacke, Hedwig Taubert, Stefan Teuchert, Barbara Textor, Vera Theissen, Christian Thelen, Walter Thiess, Susanne Thimm, Oliver Tholl, Jochen Thorn, Ulrike Thurn, Franz Thurner, Wolfgang Timm, Anita Tonini, Klaus Totzauer, Christian Träger, Friedhelm Trapp, Doris Traunspurger, Dr. Florian Triebel, Peter Tröber, Hans Ücker, Wolfgang Ulbig, Ingrid Unglert, Josef Urbanek, Ralf Urlinger, Daniela Utz, Jos van As, Wim Van Bogaert, Yves Van Vaerenbergh, Angela Venhofen, Karin Vietz, Daniela Voegt, Sascha Vogelmann, Felix Voisard, Reinhard Vrana, Johan Wadenstorfer, Carolin Waetjen, Andreas Wagenknecht, Claudia Wagenknecht, Anna Wagner, Paul Wagner, Adrienne Wallasch, Markus Wallner, Stefan Walmrath, Andreas Walter, Irina Walter, Wilhelm Wannenwetsch, Franka Weber, Kai-Adrian Weber, Manfred Weber, Silvia Weber, Andreas Wecke, Klaus Wegner, Franz Weigl, Doreen Weinhold, Verena Weiss, Ralf Weisshaar, Erik Wellner, Henrik Wenders, Klaus Wenzel, Michael Wenzel, Dr. Till Werneck, Marko Werner, Ralf Werner, Josef Westermaier, Daniela Wichary, Peter Wichmann, Wolfgang Widder, Johann Wieland, Frank Wienstroth, Magnus Wiese, Michael Wiesner, Katharina Will, Klaus Willenberg, Ludwig Willisch, Tony Wilson, Martina Wimmer, Reinhard Wimmer, Tanja Winkel, Wolfgang Winter, Ingo Wirth, Dr. Richard Wisbrun, Hinrich Wöbcken, Christine-Ilka Wolf, Peter Wolf, Jennifer Wollner, Günter Wollny, Ulrike Wortmann, Roland Wrubel, Werner Wunderlich, Albert Wuttke, Soo-Jung Youn, Werner Zach, Margarethe Zangerle, Thomas Zauber, Christoph Zeckra, Richard Zederer, Sabine Zemelka, Elfriede Zendelbach, Robert Zieglmeier, Adelheid Zimmermann, Bettina Zimmermann, Clemens Zimmermann, Thomas Zöllner, Klaus-Georg Zrenner **BMW Welt Team:** Verena Adam, Hans-Jürgen Aigner, Anja Andris, Thomas Angermeier, Petra Aubry, Patricia Bäck, Angela Bauer, Cathrin Bauer, Bernhard Baumgärtler, Hans-Jörg Begemann, Maik Beinroth, Klaus Bejenke, Petra Berchtold, Karin Beutlhauser, Nicole Bieber, Cathleen Biedermann, Christian Biester, Riccardo Blank, Werner Böck, Stefan Boes, Helmut Börner, Marius Braun, Philipp Braun, Johannes Ceh, Lùcia Maria da Silva Magalhaes, Alexander Darda, Michael Dawidziuk, Petra Deiner, Söngül Demren, Peter Dengler, Oliver Devrient, Roman Diehl, Kalina Dimitrova, Franz Dirnecker, Holger Dobben, Hermann Dollinger, Thomas Dorschner, Hichem Drissi, Stephanie Duderstadt, Rüdiger Ebel, Silvia Maria Eder, Michaela Endler, Cornelia Engel, Marion Ertel, Christian Falkinger, Dieter Feigt, Clara Fexer, Margit Fischer, Lars Freisinger, Kerstin Freitag, Martin Früchtl, Andreas Fuchs, Ulrike Gaideczka, Dörthe Gartz, Kathrin Gaude, Ivan Genov, Michaela Gilg, Wolfgang Gimpel, Vanessa Gläser, Sascha Gradl, Helga Gross, Andreas Hackbarth, Michael Hahnel, Stefanie Hamma, Klaus Hammer, Bernhard Hausmaninger, Felix Heberle, Christian

Helmke, Hans-Günther Heunisch, Andreas Hirtz, Maximilian Hoffmann, Michael Hornbacher, Renate Hörtreiter, Edmund Huber, Hanns Huber, Karl-Heinz Huber, Linda Huttary, Oualid Ibanayaden, Manuel Joseph, Manfred Junk, Monique Kaden, Seher Kalkan, Judith Karl, Ralf Kirschenmann, Daniela Kittel, Thomas Klöpfel, Judith Klöppel, Ina Knoblach, Raoul Kohler, Cornelia Kohlsdorf, Thomas Koller, Heike Kramer, Sylvia Kratz, Wolfgang Kremser, Jörg-Peter Kroll, Sebastian Kurtz, Diana Kurz, Johannes Landsperger, Margit Lange, Ulrike Lange, Christopher Leeb, Thomas Leibold, Dr. Alexander Linberg, Daniel Lo Chirco, Carolin Ludwig, Rolf Lübcke, Georgios Maskalidis, Marcelo Mastroianni, Michaela Mattejat, Katrin Mechler, Martin Megerle, Gerhard Menz, Sebastian Merkle, Stephan Milke, Carolina Mühlberger, Christian Müller, Pascal Münch, Max Niedermayer, Petra Niedermeier, Ilona Notz, Veronika Obermaier, Jos-Philip Ostendorf, Tatjana Otto, Daniel Pachner, Michael Papst, Cornelia Pätzold, Raphael Pfältzer, Wera Pfeiffer, Ute Pfungstädter, Peter Pluta, Sabrina Pluta, Hans-Joachim Pötzsch, Albrecht Proebst, Ariane Proksch, Harald Quitter, Robin Racky, Maria Rammelsberger, Ellen Reimann, Stefan Ritz, Edith Julia Rom, Michael Rößner, Bernhard Sambs, Patricia Schäfer, Britta Schenz, Matthäus Schepp, Corinna Schlögl, Maik Schmidt, Astrid Schneider, Harald Schöberl, Philipp Schuster, Rico Schwarzbach, Anja Seeck, Werner Seidel, Christine Seidl, Sven-Oliver Seitner, Christian Slowak, Stephanie Spieckermann, Sven Stadie, Angelika Stallhofer, Markus Stiefel, Linda Streicher, Judith Tabani, Alexander Tange, Turan Tarhan, Susanne Traudt, Sylvia Tresenreiter, Barbara Uelses-Turbanisch, Yvonne Uhlig, Bettina Ullerich, Salimeh Vahabzadeh, Tom van den Heuvel, Heinz Volk, Lena von Holleben, Marie Luise von Knobloch, Dr. Sibylle Beate Waegner, Ilka Waldmann, Andreas Weber, Antonia-Charlotte Weber, Gabriele Weber, Stefan Weißschädel, Rudolf Wiedemann, Anne Wiegert, Claudia Wieshuber, Karlheinz Wilder, Christian Wimmer, Franz Wimmer, Karin Wimmer, Benjamin Winkler, Silke A. Wodraschka, Markus Wolf, Sonja Wolf, Markus Zeius, Thomas Zeller, Daniel Zimmermann **boco HTS Deutschland GmbH:** Karin Böttcher, Heiner Schoenmehl **Bosch:** Rainer Becker, Rainer Eglseder, Richard Kawan, Matthias Markert, Hans-Joachim Mosch, Jörg Schirkonyer, Christian Schütz, Frank Titzenthaler, Matthias Walliser **Boston Consulting Group:** Georg Sticher **Breitsamer Entsorgung-Recycling GmbH:** Muayed-Izeldin Abdullah, Zeynei Abdullah Mohammed, Isam Jadullah Afrin, Walid Al-Rawi, Mohammed Ammar, Jamal Aso, Ahmed Assad-Zenelabedin, Muhammed Bendin, Alan Berbas, Harald Brabetz, Johann Breitsamer, Thomas Breitsamer, Ahmet Calim, Mahir Cetin, Sedat Eminov, Hans Exner, Michael Exner, Elisabeth Fredl, Karl Fredl, Sebastian Fuchs, Emrah Garip, Engin Garip, Levent Güler, Meric Güler, Damir Hadzifejzovic, Ulrich Haltmayer, Ahmed Hazar, Andreas Holladay, Huseini Husein, Tarik Jamal, Asaad Kahar, Petar Karamarkovic, Christoph Klingl, Marino Konstantin, Maik Kruhme, Marco Kulis, Yousef Mahmoud Hamed, Edris Mahmud-Hussein, Alexandra Menekse, Jörg Minkner, Remo Napionteck, Nedeljko Obradovic, Yakup Öskan, Stefan Placzek, Amarildo Prengar, Dragan Pupic, Ali Razak Reda, Saifi Saber Ali, Saad Saheb-Majid, Salar Madjid Said, Najat-Haidar Saleh, Burak Sanli, Günter Schawilye, Benjamin Smyrak, Zoran Stanojevic, Ahmad Taha Safar, Hawal Tofik, Volkan Velibeyogullari, Christian Wieder, Hadi Yildirim **Bremicker Verkehrstechnik GmbH & Co. KG:** Christian Aubeck, Herbert Döpfner **Brunner & Eisenreich:** Hans-Heinrich Dieckmann **BTB:** Karl-Heinz Völker **BTS GmbH:** Thomas Behnke **Büro für Gestaltung Wangler & Abele:** Frank Abele, Andreas Egensperger, Silvia Gagalick, Ursula Wangler **Büro + staubach gmbh Konzeption und Gestaltung:** Jan Bäse, Prof. Nils Krüger **Change Factory GmbH:** Ulrich Gerndt, Denise Maurer, Dr. Jürgen Schüppel **Christ Service GmbH:** Peter Sommer **Christian Pohl GmbH:** Michael Prinsen, Ulrich Zelter **Clauss Markisen Projekt GmbH:** Dieter Schaufler, Hans-Friedrich Schur **Climaplan:** Robert Badura, Klaus Bartenschlager, Peter Benninghoven **Comete:** Dzemal Curic, Arnold Matei **Concept Bau:** Peter Tauchen **Concept Company GmbH:** Christian Timmer **Congena:** Dr. Martin Kleibrink **Contract Division:** Francesco Paniccià **COOP HIMMELB(L)AU:** Hans Aescht, Johannes Behrens, Michael Asböck, Penelope Riba Rüttimann, Beatrix Basting, Guy Bebiè, Chris Beccone, Dominik Belzacq, Burcu Bicer, Pawel Bodzak, Carola Böker, Daniela Böttger, Verena Boyer, Iris Brandstätter, Antje Bulthaup, Timo Carl, Jan Chaldil, Ing Tse Chen, Tadeusz Chimiak, Andrea Christmann, Christoph Conradi, Alexander Couppis, Jasmin Dieterle, Claire Donnelly, Dr. Wolfdieter Dreibholz, Marion Dürnmoser, Matthias Eckardt, Caroline Ecker, Patrick Erhardt, Christian Erl, Stephan Exsternbrink, Wolfgang Fiel, Kellie Finnegan, Benedikt Frass, Doris Fritz, Edith Fritz, Helmut Frötscher, Volker Gessendorfer, Particia Gola, Gesine Görlich, Andrea Graser, Patrick Grün, Jakob Hafer, Lukas Haller, Hartmut Hank, Robert Haranza, Berit Helmecke, Markus Henning, Manfred Herrmann, Armin Hess, Marcel Hirschber, Jens Hoff, Waltraud Hoheneder, Tamas Horvath, Robert Huebser, Irakli Itonishuili, Alexander Jackson, Astrid Jagersberger, Ivana Jug, Martin Jurycz, Cynthia Kallmeyer, Gregor Kassl, Paul Kath, Areta Keller, Nicole Kirchberger, Roman Klahm, Markus Klausecker, Tobias Klein, Georg Kolmayr, Martin Konrad, Dietmar Köring, Nadine Koschke, Eva Kouteva, Quirin Krumbholz, Caroline Kufferath, Andrea Kutsche, Lorenz Lachauer, Benjamin Lange, Marion Lattenmayer, Stefan Laub, Wolfgang Leitgeb, Simon Leitner, Bernd Leopold, Charlotte Luther, Simone Mans, Mona Marbach, Marta Masternak, Andreas Mieling, Karin Miesenberger, Dennis Milam, Elke Müller, Thomas Müller, Henrike Münker, Angelika Nagel, Claudia Nehammer, Matthias Niemeyer, Martin Oberascher, Isabelle Ost, Alexander Ott, Christoph Panek, Dirk Peissl, Verena Perius, Stefan Pfefferle, Florian Pfeifer, Heinrich Pflugfelder, Markus Pillhofer, Johannes Pilz, Angelika Pöschl, Prof. Wolf D. Prix, Sandra Rankovic, Klaus Ransmayer, Jan Ravej, Ekkehard Rehfeld, Heidi Resch, Timo Rieke, Akvile Rimantaite, Goswin Rothenthal, Wolfgang Ruthensteiner, Falk Sallbach, Jasmin Sauerbier, Florian Schafschetzy, Kristina Schinegger, Ann Schirrmeister, Karolin Schmidbaur, Benjamin Schmidt, Katja Schmidt, Katharina Schneider, Patrick Schneider, Hubert Schoba, Stefan Schöch, Andrea Schöning, Andy Slusser, Anja Sorger, Gernot Stangl, Mark Steinmetz, Sigrid Steinwender, Thomas Stock, Romana Suitner, Sigrid Svensson, Helmut Swiczinsky, Kadri Tamre, Oliver Tessmann, Martina Tippelskirch, Severin Türk, Dionicio Valdez, Pascal Vauclair, Philipp Vogt, Valentin Walter, Günther Weber, Andreas Weissenbach, Renate Weissenböck, Jana Winterberg, Tom Wiscombe, Hannes Wohlgemuth, Heribert Wolfmayer, Irina Zahler, Katharina Zerlauth **CSG:** Karsten Büttner, Gerd Fischer, Steffen Schultz, Harald Überfeld **CT Creative Technology GmbH & Co KG:** Thomas Ahrens, Georg Rössler **d & h Kühllagerbau Puchheim GmbH:** Bernd Brand, Franz Drexler, Christine Hofmann, Joachim Hofmann, Karin Koch, Nadja Krauß, Simone Kronfeld, Uwe Legler, Sylvia Melzl, Manfred Putscher, Klaus Redlich, Johann Riegler, Silvio Rößler, Sven Schiller, Ralf Thiemann, Wolfgang Vetter **danpearlman markenarchitektur GmbH:** Steffen Armbruster, Thomas Barnstedt, Craig Benton, Katrin Bockholt, Anja Bonkowski, Markus Fischer, Bernd Fraerich, Nicole Gietz, Thomas Hagen, Markus Käss, Tanja Kim, Karen Klessinger, Ingo Leuschner, Hari Markus, Anja Schott, Markus Schuster, Nicole Srock Stanley, Kieran Stanley, Sven Strassner, Jan Vermehr **DAREV Engineering AG:** Karl Klein, Michael Mährlein, Andreas Pielen **das werk Berlin:** Wolf Bosse, Sebastian Schreitling **DeltaE:** Andreas Neuerer **Designfactory:** Herbert Gast, Michael Gebhart **Designfunktion:** Renate Binsch, Ines Bold, Annette Ohland, Helmut Steinbühler, Brigitte Steuernagel, Doris Walter **DeTe Immobilien:** Ulrich Dolde, Michael-Eberhard Wendler **Digicos:** Steffen Lange **Dillinger Fabrik:** Joachim Bernardi, Hans-Peter Krämer, Frank Regitz **Direktorium der Landeshauptstadt München:** Johannes Chmielewski **Do & Co Restaurants & Catering AG:** Michael Dobersberger, Attila Dogudan, Dr. Isabel Eissler, Barbara Eschbacher, Moriz Fleissinger, Dr. Stefan Hackel, Franz Hagemann, Michael Hetzler, Harald Hrastnig, Edda Kofler, Richard Müller, Ralf Pannecke, Dr. Klaus Petermann, Julia Rickens, Matthias Steinmeier, Katharina Tautschnig **Dr. Eberle & Partner Unternehmensberatung:** Dr. Rudolf Eberle **Dr. Pfeiler:** Hans Albert, Wolfgang Gollner, Sybill Kerschbaumer, Helmut Prach **DS-Managment Consulting GmbH:** Jörg von Ditfurth **DS-PLAN:** Markus Tomiak, Peter Tzeschlock **Dupont:** Holger Mertens **DWIF:** Dr. Andrea Möller, Manfred Zeiner **DYWIDAG:** Dr. Arne Berking, Otto Käsmeier **Ebener Fassaden Profiltechnik:** Manfred Zenzmeier **ECE Projektmanagement GmbH & Co. KG:** Ahmet Alkuru, Jürgen Fahrenbach, Martin Heyne, Klaus Hoffman, Ute Jürgensen, Jens Kalkbrenner, Ralf Kamprad, Ulrike Klein, Martin Lepper, Ralph Middecke, Karl-Friedrich Rauch, Dr. Martin Schubert, Josef Schüller **Eckelt Glas GmbH:** Klaus Langoth, Wolfgang Scharinger, Carmen Sulzbacher **Effertz Tore GmbH:** Oliver Burhenne, Günter Büscher, Peter Erdmann, Andreas Jansen, Klaus Kaub, Steffen Knechtel, Thomas Kohlschütter, Jens Martin, Klaus Schürmanns **Enaco:** Hermann Deckner, Anton Eisenhofer **Entenmann GmbH:** Werner E. Entenmann **EPP AG:** Josef Konzbul, Daniel Müller, Kurt Pfenninger, Pierre Scherrer,

Jean Schilb **ESPRIT Consulting:** Dr. Tobias Reisbeck **Etronixx GmbH:** Oliver Hoske, Thomas Lang, Thomas Tyborski **Eventa AG:** Florian Felsch **Evertrade GmbH:** Yehoshua Chmiel, Roland Fein, Christian Hafner, Pessia Magén, Birgit Schlosser **Expolab:** Ferdinand Albrecht, Katharina Berres, Jan Füchtjohann, Pat Kalt, Brigid Meredith, Peter Scholler, Sophie Seidenath, Christian Seidl, Alexander Strub **Fachpreisrichter BMW Welt Architekturwettbewerb:** Prof. Dr. Marc Angélil, Prof. Dietmar Eberle, Prof. Dietrich Fink, Prof. Dr. Gunter Henn, Prof. Peter Kulka, Prof. Ulrike Lauber, Prof. Christiane Thalgott, Michael Triebswetter, Konrad Wohlhage **FEUER Kommunikation und Design AG:** Boris Dolkhani, Florian Herrmann, Matthias Meier-Stuckenberger **FG stijl:** Colin Finnegan, Gerard Glintmeijer **Fieger Lamellenfenster GmbH:** Matthias Ficht **Fliesen Röhlich:** Lothar Abert, Murat Demircan, Mehmet Er, Markus Fischer, Stefan Hacker, Herbert Hölzel, Arnold Juri, Tobias Mittrach, Christian Müller, Martin Röhlich, Franz Schutzbier, Roland Tangermann, Andreas Trenn, Roland Wöhrle **Flughafen München GmbH:** Gerald Appelt, Corinna Born, Wolfgang Inderwies, Florian Pötsch, Birgit Riede, Winrich Stoerner, Michael Zierer **FM Global:** Klaus Thierbach, Angela Weiss **fmDrive:** Reinhard Albang, Josef Bergmann, Özlem Bozkurt, Julia Brennauer, Andreas Brüggenthies, Tammo Buhren, Erkan Celik, Mai Dang-Goy, Albrecht Ehlers, Martin Feldner, Sebastian Flint, Tobias Förster, Christian Frisch, Carsten Gramlow, Florian Gründel, Gerry Hauck, Hans-Ulrich Hilpert, Suada Kadric, Heidi Kaiser, Ayse Kedik, Barbara Köhler, Harald Kössl, Michael Kunitsch, Klaus Kuttenhofer, Abbas Kuzucu, Dirk Luthe, Herbert Lütkestratkötter, Dieter Müller, Tanja Müller, Ulli Napp, Machmout Pechlivan, Arnulf Piepenbrock, Ulli Schillinger, Thomas Schmidt, Silvio Schwellnuss, Songül Seyatoglu, Elana Siberski, Ralf Smolka, Alexandra Sunkel, Gunther Trautmann **Fotodesign Buck:** Marcus Buck **4 Wheels Servie + Logistik GmbH:** Robin Vogl **Fournell Showtechnik GmbH:** André Fournell **Franken + Kiening GbR:** Christoph Kiening **Fräs- & Strahltechnik Ltd., Ingoldstadt:** Fethi Cay, Ayhan Müllbauer, Björn Schecklmann, Peter Schecklmann **Freier Architekt:** Klaus Beutler, Thomas Gerstmeir **FRENER & REIFER Metallbau, Brixen:** Franz Ballerstaller, Timo Bühlmeister, Klaus Fenners, Michael Fischnaller, Georg Frener, Konrad Gasser, Carsten Haedge, Christoph Hilpold, Josef Hilpold, Stefan Krebs, Hans-Jürgen Lierenz, Alexander Lorenz, Wolfgang Ludwig, Florian Mair, Leo Mair, Frank Osanna, Armin Pichler, Markus Plieger, Gerhard Ploner, Michael J. Purzer, Andreas Puzicki, Renate Ratiu, Andreas Reifer, Bernhard Reifer, Franz Reifer, Michael Reifer, Matthias Schrott, Markus Überbacher **Friends+Friends:** Sven Stimac **Fritsch Gerüstbau GmbH:** Franz Floßmann, Peter Miller, Uwe Neugebauer, Herbert Patzina, Walter Reichelt **Ftronik:** Dr. Karl de Molina **Fugentechnik Hösel, München:** Manfred Hösel **G. Schmitz:** Norbert Berger, Gertrud Bojer, Ireneusz Branski, Branko Coskovic, Alois Danzl jr., Jürgen Fischer, Mehmet Gökbayir, David Hiller, Mergim Kuci, Werner Maurer, Kassim Mwapembe-Jaffari, Günter Rahmsdorf, Hans Jürgen Schmitz-Senge, Josef Schwaiger, Manfred Vlasak, Hans Weiss **G. Theodor Freese GmbH:** Wilfried Schlenker **Gahrens + Battermann GmbH:** Markus Busch, Sebastian Schulze **gap Gesellschaft für Autopflege mbH:** Kai Dierdorf, Werner Hieber, Wolfgang Hieber **gate 11:** Arnd Buss von Kuk, Julian Fischer, Axel Flachenegger, Iris Hausmann, Christian Künstler, Maria Ploskow, Daniel Stacherdinger, Conny Unger, Daniela Wilke **Gerhard Schmidt & Partner:** Katharina Moss, Gregor Spengler **Gerling Consulting Gruppe:** Jens Kaltbeitzer **GHMT:** Viachaslau Shyfryn **Gillhuber Logistik + Dienste:** Karl-Heinz Hainmüller **GKK Dialog Group:** Andreas Brinkmann, Robert Gräßler, Sven Griffel, Harald Kling, Roman Kretzer, Wolfgang Krug, Björn Nauheimer, Markus Pöttinger **Glöckl-Gebäudereinigungs GmbH:** Michaela Witzany **Goldmann:** Margarete Goldmann **Grinbold Metallbau Unterbissingen:** Georg Grinbold **Gruber:** Michael Gruber **Grunwald GmbH & Co. KG:** Jörg Buob, Frank Dworsky, Marcus Gebler, Hannelore Grunwald, Edith Hochrein, Michael Mandl, Angelika Steiger **Guth Design:** Uli Guth **H&T Verlags GmbH Co. KG:** Christian Stengl **Häfele:** Herbert Messmann, Stefan Sauer **Hans Lechner ZT-GmbH:** Susanne Danzmeyer Beyrl, Sabine Ebster, Christian Ellmeier, Horst Fuchs, Dietmar Gobitzer, Andreas Haiderer, Tayana Hergarden, Herbert Kanov, Emanuel Krause, Walter Kräutler, Hans Lechner, Sabine Liebenau, Martina Roj, Michael Scherz, Jan Schubert, Babette Schwarz, Michaela Summer, Christian Szeglat, Elfriede Tösch, Andreas Winterstein, Nina Wohlrab, Daniela Zupan **Hauptmann & Kompanie Werbeagentur:** David Hauptmann, Cornelia Hepting **Helbling:** Kurt Gantenbein, Benno Wyss **Heller und Partner:** Lutz Eckardt, Dr. Stephan Heller **HEPS GmbH:** Dieter Aschenbrenner, Josef Aster, Klaus-Dieter Böhme, Cosmo D´Anolfo, Mike Ficker, Torsten Fischer, Herbert Gehrmann, Peter Grashuber, Georg Hasler, Stefanie Heps, Josef Holzmüller, Roland Kamin, Ernst Köhler, Michael Krumpel, Franz Lehner, Horst Löser, Osman Memeti, Halil Milak, Lars Mudrow, Enrico Pfeiffer, Helmut Preis, Andreas Ruml, Mario Schuman, Sven Theelke, Johann Treffer, Roland Tschaschke, Eckard Witt **Herbert Rapp GmbH & Co.:** Thomas Mann **Hochkant Film GmbH:** Gernot Aschoff, Stefanie Biegelmann, Pascal Bohlen, Dieter Deventer, Diana Drews, Akira Endo, Fabian Fischer, Doerte Kaschub, Dörte Kaschub, Oliver Kochs, Josch Kretzschmar, Ingmar Lange, Christian Lonk, Werner Maritz, Tobias Müller, Peter Refle, Florian Seiler, Henning Stirner, Manuel Wenger **HTS Deutschland GmbH & Co. KG:** Wilfried Bayer, Albert Brecht, Marcus Schilk, Heiner Schönmehl **Hubertus Hamm:** Hubertus Hamm, Tatjana Kunath, Lisa Kerp, Jan Schünke **IRW Aktiengesellschaft Beratende Ingenieure:** Michael Goronczy **IB Bensch:** Georg Bensch **IB Blei:** Christian Blei **IB Brunner:** Thomas Brunner **IB Ecke:** Gerd Ecke **IB Emmerling:** Yvonne Bauer, Hubert Emmerling, Andreas Wallner **IB Fichtner + Köppl:** Johann Bleiziffer, Dr. Johann Köppl, Christian Ramsteiner **IB Franke:** Dieter Götz, Klaus Peter Greithaner **IB Henning:** Gerhard Henning **IB Hoffmann:** Frank Brunz, Patrick Fries, Peter Gothe, Armin Hoffmann **IB K.-D. Berndt:** Klaus-Dietmar Berndt **IB Kretschmer:** Werner Kretschmer **IB Lehner:** Günther Lehner, Werner Müller **IB Martini:** Bernd Martini **IB Muck:** Andreas Bügel, Klaus Lenard, Walter Muck, Gunnar Müller-Langecker, Thomas Sandner, Wolfgang Schießl, Hartmut Siegl **IB Mühlberger:** Jörg Schnittger **IB PSS:** Dagmar Müller, Harald Päßler, Jochen Peters, Frank Pfeiffer, Manfred Schüßler, Dieter Seitz, Norbert Sperr, Jürgen Strauß, Erika Ungar **IB Rosenzopf:** Thomas Rosenzopf **IBG Automation GmbH:** Matthias Goeke **IBM Business Consulting Services:** Dr. Markus Altmeier, Markus Altmeier, Harald Baumeister, Andreas Britsche, Hans-Hagen Didjurgeit, Karl Dietrich, Axel Dimroth, Carsten Eickhoff, Klaus Fernholz, Tilmann Flum, Matthias Hanitsch, Ralf Herzig, Martin Hess, Elmar Husmann, Federico Juettner, Britta Knappe, Michael Köhler, Stefan Kramer, Armin Malik, Andreas Marholz, Dr. Rainer Mehl, Uwe Mertens, Uwe Müller, Tarek Nouri, Dr. Claus Ørum Hansen, Jörg Peine, Carsten Pingel, Stephan Rahmede, Stefan Roth, Alexander Schneider, Anita Schuldt, Frank Weier, Markus Winkler, Ingo Winkler, Norbert Wölfel, Marion Zeindl **ict AG:** Rainer Armbruster, Jörg Bader, Jochen Bauch, Michael Bohnert, Alexander Bommel, Susanne Dietz, Manfred Dolde, Klaus Dost, Josef Fetscher, Alexander Frink, Hans Goller, Martin Hahnenkamp, Karl Hartmann, Franz Huber, Andreas Jud, Helmut Kienast, Maike Kruse, Harald Kurz, Michael Lachmann, Andrea Lehr, Mike Mader, Alexander Mings, Daniel Ocker, Maximilian Paulus, Sybille Pohlner, Jürgen Riecker, Carmen Schoen, Alexander Straub, Michael Trost, Tobias Wondra, Tobias Wurster **Imaginary Forces:** Chip Houghton, Saffron Kenny, Frederic Liebert, Mikon van Gastel, Lisa Villamil **IMIXS GmbH:** Helmut Gruber, Dr. Brigitte Mayr, Volker Probst **IMO Leipzig:** Mathias Blaschke, Robert Eymann, Enrico Funke, Uwe Jacobi, Gerd Lieschke, Bernd Rudolph, Andreas Schimmel, Jörg Steinbach **Ingenieurbüro Nusko:** Franziska Dendorfer, Robert Dendorfer, Veronika Gerber, Franz Gernbauer, Stephan Horn, Günter Loest, Gisela Marschall, Victor Nenadovych, Hendrik Opitz, Oswald Ruhl, Niklas Stepper, Thomas Wenk **Ingenieurbüro Schönenberg + Partner, München:** Rüdiger Schönenberg, Jiri Vesely **Ingolstädter Autohaus GmbH:** Friedrich Hofmann **InPool Kommunikationstechnik GmbH:** Peter In **Interbrand Zintzmeyer & Lux GmbH:** Gerd Burla, Helga Capitaine, Tilman Fuchs, Lena Kessel, Christian Lungershausen, Christof Macke, Christoph Marti, Metin Seyrek, Roger Sonanini, Christopher Wünsche **InterCad GbR:** Dirk Schoner **Interna srl:** Fabio Ceroi **Interna srl:** Uliana Gianluca, Chiara Mattarollo, Diego Travan **International-Business-Communication:** Linda Goodwin-Huber-Wilhelm **Interone GmbH:** Nancy Bachmann, Christian Basche, Anja Baumeister, Claudia Beckh, Lorena Beltrami, Heinz Blei, Hans Brückner, Sven Busse, Kerstin Buchkremer, Caroline Daamen, Ilka Ehlers, Carolin Feicht, Thomas Feldhaus, Lars Gerckens, Sabrina Gleiss, Thomas Gleißner, Alexander Gloning, Tobias Graser, Lissy Gross, Matthias Grunert, Thorsten Harders, Susanne Heigl, Barbara Heinemann, Philip Hertel, Christoph Hoidn, Georg Klemm, Holger Knauer, Jan Köpke, Guntram Kopp, Kalle Kormann, Siegmund Lienhard, Sandra Lipka, Jan-Peter Lübcke, Katrin Markworth, Marian Masa, Jascha Müller, Wolfang Müller, Holger Nauen, Sylvi Nilsson,

Claudia Nohl, Jens Pastyrik, Max Plötz, Nadja Ringel, Serdar Sahin, Florian Schleuppner, Robert Schulke, Oliver Schwank, Michael Schwarz, Claudia Schwingen, Hannes Stockner, Martin Studemund, Silja Stuhlmann, Philipp von Essen, Michael Wald, Philipp Walter, Jochen Weidner, Andreas Wellhausen, Tobias Wortmann **InVision Software AG:** Jens Keilen, Marco Leven, Dr. Volker Oshege, Christoph Rütte, Manuel Schulz **IT Demands:** Oliver Kilb **ITK:** Torsten Breitel **Jack Rouse Associates:** James Keith **Jannet IT Services:** Markus Bentrup **Jansen Brandschutz Tore:** Norbert Hackmann, Josef Hager, Hans-Jürgen Knott, Uwe Schmidt **JG GmbH:** Bernd Altmann, Helmut Bahmann, Orhan Bajrami, Werner Bamberger, Alfred Bauer, Matthias Benning, Elke Burdack, Rainer Deininger, Marco Dinale, Rolf Dittbrenner, Susanne Egger, Erwin Englert, Kathrin Ertelt, Thomas Feifel, Detlef Fellwock, Bodo Fienke, Leonard Fink, Dr. Armin Franke, Stefan Gabel, Gerhard Gerstmayr, Jürgen Gutknecht, Wilfried Gutstein, Stefan Haase, Sabine Hitzler, Otto Hörbrand, Turan Karakus, Uli Kirschbaum, Stefan Kloker, Franz Korschinsky, Bernd Kuschmieder, Dieter Lange, Josef Langenmaier, Siegmar Linder, Michael List, Richard Löffler, Dieter Lohner, Elke Lohner, Walter Lohner, Viktor Merenda, Bernd Moser, Bernd Noack, Bernd Pohlers, Michael Prozenko, Alois Reif, Erwin Renner, Georg Ritter, Daniel Sattler, Rainer Sattler, Monika Schröttle, Vinzenz Seifried, Josef Steidle, Reinhard Strobel, Wilhelm Süß, Eugen Tausend, Henry Wagner, Wilfried Wagner, Franz Wais, Xaver Waldmann, Silke Weber, Angelika Weng, Christian Winter, Thomas Wioncek, Jochen Zander **Johnson Controls Systems & Service GmbH:** Klaus Abraham, Johann Anneser, Slavomir Bak, Michael Busert, Ursula Denecke, Jens Doepelheuer, Miroslav Foitzik, Mike Gelfert, Wolfgang Heimerl, Werner Hoerl, Eugen Jakszlowicz, Bernhard Jokiel, Markus Jokiel, Sven Kaiser, Helmut Karl, Steve Koeppen, Antoni Kojak, Josef Konarski, Joachim Kroha, Peter Kroll, Alexander Kronthaler, Lutz Krusche, Edward Majewski, Krzysztof Mazur, Guenther Mehler, Jerszy Monczak, Roland Otrebski, Horst Pelzl, Johann Piser, Rudi Podafka, Thomas Promberger, Barbara Rech, Michael Rees, Alexander Schaedel, Robert Scheibl, Christian Schimitzek, Tobias Schoeger, Todensz Soboczyk, Marian Szponar, Peter Ulm, Michael Wolfrum **K+B E-Tech:** Johannes Bricha, Günter Gebhard, Alexander Gerl, Franz Hausner, Klaus Heigl, Christian Huber, Martin Irrgang, Josef Kappenberger jun., Thomas Kappenberger, Franz Kistler, Franz Kolbeck, Michael Krause, Stefan Laub, Klaus Laumer, Thomas Lemberger, Johann Lex, Robert Lodwig, Waldemar Matejko, Andrzej Nowakoski, Josef Röckl, Franz Scheuerer, Stefan Schmid, Richard Serve, Thomas Stockerl, Stefan Wagner, Max Wanninger, Werner Zellmer, Martin Zwicknagl **KAEFER Industrie GmbH:** Ivan Buhuvac, Richard Bukato, Markus Fürstenberg, Pavel Juklicek, Marco Klaric, Hans-Jörg Pirngruber, Manfred Rakowski, Hans Weber **KAMPERder BAU GmbH:** Bernhard Uedl **Karl Lausser GmbH:** Josef Adam, Stefan Aich, Heinz Anleitner, Johannes Anleitner, Heribert Attenberger, Rainer Backert, Martin Baumann, Frank Beetz, Huy Bui, Ella Deuschl, Martin Eisenschink, Dominik Foierl, Werner Götz, Michael Gruber, Norbert Gruber, Erwin Heigl, Herbert Hilmer, Peter Hoffmann, Herbert Immich, Udo Jahn, Stefan Kaiser, Gerhard Kleebauer, Gottfried Kleebauer, Thomas Kögl, Jörg Kögler, Uwe Korb, Werner Korb, Michael Kronfeldner, Mario Künzel, Heribert Lausser, Karl Lausser, Karl-Heinz Lausser, Ralf Lausser, Manfred Lehner, Bernd Liebl, Alfons Loibl, Johannes Mühlbauer, Detlef Nickchen, Uwe Olschewski, Irene Pflügl, Erwin Poiger, Robert Prommesberger, Peter Reißmann, Michael Rosenhammer, Dieter Rothaug, Josef Sagstetter, Dominik Schiedeck, Mario Schmelchel, Matthäus Söllheim, Josef Spießl, Günther Träger, Josef Wänninger, Robert Wendling, Olaf Wiedemann, Albert Wittmann, Markus Zimmermann, Wolfgang Zollner **KEMAS GmbH:** Peter Vogel **Kersken & Kirchner:** Thilo Hoffmann, Susan Jurisch **Kersken + Kirchner GmbH:** Thilo Hoffmann **Kiessmann + Ziehn:** Hans-Georg Kiessmann **KIM - Kölner Institut für Managementberatung:** Barbara Ahrens, Stephan Holtmeier, Daniela Settels **K-IS GmbH:** Dr. Alfred Heszheimer, Marcell Kießig, Uwe Muck **Klostermair Messebau:** Elke Auernhammer, Georg Birkmeir, Karin Eubel, Ralph Fritzsche, Robert Glombitza, Margitta Helbig, Maren Kall, Anneliese Karmann, Anita Klingenstein, Klaus Klostermair, Helga Schlingmann, Rainer Stehle, Luz Unger, Daniel Walter, Stefan Wittmayr **Knöller Fußbodentechnik:** Olaf Ficker, Michael Megerle, Peter Mikus, Alfred Otto, Martin Otto, Marco Plößl, Andre Schoder **Kommatec:** Steffen Rausch, Fabian Scholz **Konzeptbüro Wessel:** Alexandra Kohl, Ingo Wessel **Kothig GmbH:** Thomas Gebler, Andreas Göbl, Jürgen Hagesmeier, Sigi Heckmeier, Franz Kienzl, Walter Kothig, Jerzy Lakotta, Franz Merz, Hubert Nespithal, Benno Pedziwiatr, Dieter Probst, Rudolf Ruedell, Achim Rust, Thomas Samol, Thomas Schachtner, Alfred Schwarzmann, Martina Stieglmair, Johanna Waldbart, Herbert Wurzer **Krantz TKT Brandschutztechnik:** Denny Baucza, Michaela Baumann, Klaus Binsteiner, Steffen Böttcher, Nikolaos Fotiadis, Horst Frohnrath, Detlef Geserick, Olaf Goyn, Carla Gründer, Walter Haas, Dr. Klaus Hermsdorf, Karl Hettwer, Andreas Höhne, Jens Jarschel, Helmut Kachel, Erkki Kallunki, Holger Keßel, Roberto Killermann, Rüdiger Kirstätter, Helge Klotke, Michael-Frank Lamle, Burghard Nähter, Jürgen Neisner, Steffen Neubert, Faustino Pena, Michael Pommer, Rudolf Radler, Michael Rosche, Johannes Rost, Horst Rostalski, Klaus Rüter, Holger Schmidt, Uwe Schubert, Werner Sehm, Peter Siegmund, Jens Stolze, Miklos Vachter, Uwe Wagner, Rolf Warmuth, Rainer Witte, Frank Wundke, Michael Zimmer **Kuehn Bauer Partner:** Mandy Adam, Werner Bauer, Jochen Bergmeier, Michael Brach, Nils Brandstätter, Petra Brunk, Nicole Finkbeiner, Günther Hammitzsch, Ulrike Ibbach, Brigitte Kaiser, Erika Kuehn, Michael Kuehn, Michael Kuehn jr., Jürgen Manger, Christine Meyr, Jörg Mundle, Rita Mundle, Katrin Ozimek, Siegfried Roswadowski, Richard Sagner, Reinhold Schuler, Thomas Thienel, Anne-Kristin Volz, Johanna Wiesheu **Kühlanlagenbau Süd-Ost GmbH:** Jens Ertelt, Falko Goettert, Daniel Heinrich, Andreas Kluttig, Torsten Menzel, Bernd Riel, Werner Rößler, Nils Schwager **LAMILUX Heinrich Strunz GmbH:** Frank Buchsbaum, Alexander Murin, Jürgen Schmidt **Landeshauptstadt München:** Peter Bachmeier, Georg Dunkel, Andreas Gaisbauer, Thomas Holz, Horst Mentz, Franz Meyer, Abdil Öztürk, Jerzy Petlicki, Maximilian Pusl, Michael Schaller, Bernd Schmidbaur, Peter Seitz, Klaus Späth, Karl Thiem, Christian Ude, Christof Warislohner, Roland Zeller **Landeshauptstadt München. Referat für Arbeit und Wirtschaft:** Rudolf Boneberger **Lang + Burkhardt Verkehrsplanung und Städtebau:** Michael Angelsberger, Till Burkhardt **Lang-Holz-Rasch:** Rebecca Henke, Dirk Rasch **Lehn Fotodesign:** Bernhard Lehn **LGA Nürnberg:** Wolfgang Pöllmann-Heller **Lightpower GmbH:** Bertram Czeczka, Markus Drewniok, Stefan Fiedler, Franz Josef Wewer, Ralph Jörg Wezorke **Lindner AG:** Andrea Bartlsperger, Tom Bührig, Johann Felixberger, Stefan Frank, Carmen George, Marcel Glöß, Werner Gugg, Roger Hadek, Thomas Kraus, Josef Kriegl, Willfried Napirei, Falk Neidhardt, Jürgen Nestler, Daniel Neumann, Jens Nillius, Andre Polansky, Tom Rehwagen, Sven Reichelt, Mathäus Reichl, Wolfgang Reinhard, Ulrich Rettler, Michael Schene, Martin Sieber, Andreas Sommerfeld, Lisane Sommerfeld, Michael Stache, Andre Ukley, Robby Väth, Ulrich Winter, Jens Ziegenbalg, Marcel Zielke **Luci P:** Stephanie Thon, Tina Maria Werner **lucidmusic:** Azhar Kamal **Ludwig Tobler KG:** Ulrike Engelhardt, Martina Kubny **Lummel:** Gotfried Behr, Alfred Döll, Werner Ebert, Lothar Gebel, Anton Hein, Georg Lummel, Heinz Lummel, Stefan Lummel, Christian Neumann, Michael Schaupp, Hubert Schmitt, Matthias Völker, Horst Wehner, Iris Wehner **MAB:** Alexander Kerkow, Ninon Schuster, Peter Stroeh **Magna Steyr:** Oliver Frech, Dr. Gerhard Grill-Kiefer, Martin Hillbrand, Stephan Kostwein, Peter Kriegl **Makon GmbH:** Günter Kopp, Rüdiger Limpert, Markus Messerschmidt **Management Zentrum St. Gallen - Consulting & Education:** Ludwig W. Allgoewer **Manpower GmbH & Co. KG:** Nicole Aichele **MARITIM TV:** Jochen Herbst, Andreas Juranits, Maximilian Neumayer, Thorsten Schmitz, Werner von Heybowitz, Dagmar Werther **Matrix:** Wolfgang Lechner, Ferdinand Mahr **Maurer Söhne GmbH & Co. KG:** Esat Alatas, Wolfgang Amberg, Frank Bertling, Jörg Beutler, Johannes Bolz, Manfred Daurer, Dietmar-Jens Filipp, Andreas Fritzsche, Georg Gruber, Klaus Hahn, Thomas Hahn, Günther Heiss, Klaus Hilpert, Gerd Hockerdt, Thomas Hockes, Klaus Holler, Manfred Josef, Herbert Jung, Karoly Kesztyüs, Oliver Lampalzer, Andreas Mann, Gunter Matschinsky, Cornelia Meyer, Thomas Möckl, Uwe Möller, Wolfgang Molz, Horst Mucha, Frank Müller, Michael Müller-Lanzl, Michael Munschke, Alexander Neumann, Ramonchito Olavydez, Christoph Ostermeier, Helmut Paul, Josef Recht, Reiner Reiff, Günter Riedl, Ronald Sauer, Andreas Schaller, Thomas Seifert, Stjepan Skalicki, Vitus Strähuber, Marica Tikvic, Roland Uhlmann, Jalcim Ünalan, Klaus Vogt, Stefan Wagner, Jochen Wehrle, Peter Wochnik, Rolf Wolter, Jürgen Zaus **MAX.SENSE Live Marketing:** Michael Brohm **May:** Antonio Augieri, Rosario Gueli, Rüdiger Hadatsch, Simon Hellmeier, Dimitri Kaufmann, Christoph May, Birgit Müller, Christian Nass, Jens Neumann, Otto Rosenberger **Mayr:** Karl Mayr **MDS:** Jens Swadzba **Mediaplus:** Wolfgang Bauersachs, Marion Brandl, Christian Kaessmann, Nicole Merheim **Metallbau Schubert:** Norman Eisold, Alexander Jantke,

Hagen Klimke, Klaus Pogontke, Reiner Schubert **metron GmbH:** Johann Bauer, Robert Billinger, Thomas Grübl, Josef Hirsch, René Kunze, Ronald Kunze, Martin Lauerer, Gerhard Loibl, Paul Lorenz, Jürgen Maier, Jens Meisner, Frank Mikolaiczyk, Thomas Petric, Markus Reinhardt, Norbert Schneider, Angela Stautner **MG Ingenieure:** Mathias Gabel **MINI München:** Helmut Käs, Gustav Richter **MKG events:** Rainer Krug **MKT AG:** Maik Altmann, Roland Berens, Werner Bleier, Peter Braasch, Benno Burger, Zarko Cupic, Angelos Danis, Enrico Donath, Nikolaus Frecot, Karl Frey, Manfred Geitner, Hans Grinsch, Peter Haschkamp, Volker Häss, Martin Hatzl, Matthias Höft, Michèle Janssen, Christian Kerth, Christian Klause, Christian Kraus, Josef Kraut, Manfred Lechner, Antonio Melillo, Michele Melillo, Georg Menzel, Markus Miller, Christian Mohapel, Martin Munder, Thomas Neumeier, Miroslav Pavlata, Christine Penkert, Richard Penkert, Ferdinand Pfeil, Franz Pohmann, Helmut Raum, Christian Rublack, Hans Schweinester, Ratko Stevanovic, Alexa Stippel, Michael Thome, Wolfgang Wilkes **modus x:** Reinhard Wespel **msg systeme:** Markus Binder, Herbert Lindner, Hardy Oppmann, Dr. Michael Schreyer, Wolfgang Schüßler, Hilmar Schwarz, Bernd Völker **muenchen.de:** Marc Bozigursky **Münchener Stadrundfahrten oHG:** Franziska Huber, Alice Weissauer **Mundal Fenster- und Fassadentechnik GmbH:** Franz Fischer, Hugo Kloker **MyProcess:** Rene Kretzschmar **NAT AG:** Brigitte Brandstetter, Ingrid Hetz, Branislav Lukovic, Leonhard Meiler, Aristidis Orfanidis, Jürgen Richers, Thomas Scheck, Markus Urbainski **new direction GmbH:** Klaudia Kolenda-Jarosch, Stephan Weber **Nexolab:** Philip Eller, Christoph Krzikalla, Robert Megerle, Bernd Mersdorf, Ilona Notz, Bela Peterson, Armin Ritter, Christian Schamberger, Christian Schauler, Axel Schweigert, Simon Spelthahn, Brigitte Waibl, Uwe Zybell **Nomen International Deutschland GmbH:** Gregor Rotter **Oberndörfer Grafik GmbH:** Fritz Oberndörfer, Heinz Oberndörfer **Ogilvy&Mather:** Florentina Claus, Daniela Friedel, Simon Oppmann, Peter Roemmelt, Roland Stauber **OgilvyOne:** Steffen Busse, Dorothea Feurer, Andrea Goebel, Volker Helm, Bettina Josting, Vivian Kempf, Antje König, Heiko Krassmann, Sabrina M. Krumpa, Tanja Langstrof, Zinga Makumbundu, Saman Rahmanian, Parand Rohani, Annette Rust, Ulf Schmidt, Bejadin Selimi, Heiner Vogelmann, Thorsten Voigt **Olympiapark München GmbH:** Stephan Braun, Julia Finsterbusch, Arno Hartung, Alice Kilger, Tobias Kohler, Melanie Listl, Franz Nagel, Wilfrid Spronk **Orru Projektierung und Fassadentechnik:** Mirko Erkenbrecher, Michael Orru **Oswald Design:** Bettina Oswald **Otto Christ AG Waschanlagen:** Peter Bros, Werner Duda, Manfred Kretzinger, Manfred Krötzsch, Maurus Schäfer **Outokumpu GmbH:** Jochen Ziegler **P+R Park & Ride GmbH:** Frank Zöttl **Paley & Partner Sp. z o.o.:** Zdzilaw Budek, Jazek Chaczykowski, Artur Furgal, Kazimierr Groniekie, Stanislaw Guzak, Tomasz Mardyla, Eugeniusz Ryba **panTerra.tv:** Michael Dehner, Herbert Fischer, Sarah Huppmann, Andreas Stigler **Panzer GmbH:** Karin Scherer **Paul Schmidt Aufzüge:** Werner Adam, Walter Althaus, Holger Beine, Reiner Brück, Armin Bürkle, Stefan Eiden, Bernd Evers, Michael Evers, Burkard Franke, Wolfgang Geiling, Sabine Golz, Helmut Grebe, Wilfried Guntermann, Ralf Hänsch, Klemens Harbecke, Jürgen Hartmann, Robert Hilmers, Peter Hilse, Heinrich Hoffmeister, Peter Huneck, Harald Kaiser, Willi Kaiser, Wolfgang Kaiser, Lothar Kaufmann Schmid, Oskar Kempel, Klaus Dieter Müller, Mathias Müller, Donald Pogremno, Andreas Ricken, Josef Rohden, Herbert Schäfer, Werner Schäfer, Karl Heinz Schnurbus, Christoph Schröder, Horst Schumacher, Jürgen Weber, Tobias Welticke, Otto Werth, Karl Heinz Wienand, Willi Wienand, Markus Wieners, Bernd Wienhold, Jürgen Zimmermann, Detlef Zühlke **pbb planungsbüro balke:** Elisabeth Balke, Natascha Balke, Cordelia Drescher, Didem Hazar, Gerald Holler, Manuela Kozinovic, Doreen Pohle **PCE:** Erwin Barthel, Hubert Bauer, Göksel Günes, Jochen Kohl, Roland Köhler, Manuel Kuhn, Gottfried Kürbiß, Heiko Leistner, Jürgen Mais, Burkhard Rottmann, Bernd Ruf, Markus Schlereth, Felix Schmitt, Dirk Schreiter, Werner Sendner **PENTA GmbH:** Sonja Bacher, Petra Holocher, Leonardo Lutilsky, Petra Zandtner **Permasteelisa:** Ivan Bortoluzzi, Stefania De Luca, Ferderico Liberali, Monica Marin, Marzio Perin, Mauro Zanchin **Peter / K+Z:** Andreas Peter **Philosys:** Peter Göb, Michael Plass **Plan.Net:** Sebastian Donat **Planungsbüro Balke:** Joachim Billinger **Planungsbüro Stahlbau:** Siegfried Haunerdinger **player & franz studio:** Alexander Plajer **plus service GmbH TÜV Süd:** Sebastian Bernt, Thomas Fischer **PMS Projektmanagement Services GmbH:** Günther Weber **Poltrona Frau:** Matteo Bernocchi, Alberto Gullini **procon IT:** Helmut Braun, Rainer Eberhard, Günther Langer, Hans-Jürgen Reggel **PRO-Elektroplan GmbH:** Josef Emmer, Peter Feike, Petra Hartmann, Johannes Heuwieser, Lucia Ho, Angelika Kahnt, Peter Kovacz, Dorothea Kuzora, Bernhard Lohmann, Karl-Heinz May, Christine Müller, Robert Rapp, Bernd Ropeter, Alexandra Weber **Progeo:** Markus Motte **PSG:** Holger Agotai, Holger Pothmann, Arthur Rösch **Puchner & Schum:** Bernd Callsen, Nicol Puchner **Pupeter:** Josef Altmann, Roland Asam, Petar Bozanovic, Wolfgang Dallinger, Ibrahim Demir, Sinan Demir, Karl Haidinger, Bernd Hartnigk, Petar Keskic, Patrycjusz Krawczyk, Robert Lichtenstern-Spevan, Eduard Perek, Helmut Sauer, Konrad Schnotz, Jörg Schröder, Petar Sliscovic, Necip Solmaz, Georg Strupf, Senad Ticevic, Willi Träger, Dietmar Treppe, Hans Witzel, Adam Wollnik, Martin Wulke, Artur Zans, Peter Zans **PWC Consulting:** Frank Weier **q-mon Consulting:** Daniel Butscher, Dr. Jens Saadhoff **Qualit Op:** Franz Kammler **Training-Beratung-Konzeption:** Rainer Wacke **realgrün Landschaftsarchitekten:** Ute Andreas, Wolf D. Auch, Ulrike Böhm, Stephan Huber, Manfred Kerler, Klaus Neumann, Eva Prasch **Rechtsanwälte Wagensonner Luhmann Breitfeld Helm:** Dr. Götz Mezger **Reger Studios GmbH:** Jochen Biagosch, Christian Bleninger, Veit Benedict Friedrich, Nicole Führer, Thomas Heinemann, Siggi Hussner, Vlado Kovacevic, Daniel Kriesl, Tanja Kugler, Thomas Maurer, Menan Mirtoski, Diarmuid O'Brien, Markus Reger, Manuela Schatte, Anja Schwartz, Thomas Steger **Reinhardt & Ahrens GbR:** Thomas Macht **Reisacher GmbH:** Peter Alexander Reisacher **RetoWorks:** Reto Keller **Rhein-Neckar:** Oskar Donhauser, Jürgen Gaidzick, Florian Grassmann, Klaus Heilmann, Willi Hense, Viktor Meier, Matthias Weik, Hans Wirl, Ronald Wirl, Syle Zena **Richard Schulz Tiefbau:** Davide Alexandre Marques, Carlos Manuel Antunes da Silva, Josef Biro, Herbert Dreyßig, Edmund Fuchs, Maximilian Greller, Josef Groitl, Nicole Helmer, Stanomir Mitic, Manuel Pires Esteves, Daniel Reinhardt, Mario Schmidt, Steffen Scholz, Mario Schuhmacher, Muy Sopjani, Matthias Zorn **Richter GmbH:** Rolf Richter **Riller & Schnauck GmbH:** Sven Rabe, André Reiser **Roland Kuffler GmbH:** Roland Kuffler **Rolf Horn GmbH:** Dirk Horn **Rompe Design Jobfashion GmbH & Co. KG:** Susanne Rompe, Johannes Viethen **RTT:** Alexander Barth, Maria Glas, Jochen Hegewald, Christoph Karrasch, Florian Köhler, Otmar Kratzer, Christiane Lantermann, Reinhard Meier, Thomas Orenz, Vivien Schreiber, Sabine Siegl **SAINT ELMO'S:** Julia Bistrick, Arnd Feuerbaum, Ulrike Glöckler, Isabel Klose, Christoph Liebl, Christoph Sackerer, Thomas Satori, Eva Scharnhorst, Alexander Thomas Späth, Lucy Westermair **Sales Concept:** Heinrich Wickinghoff **Salzbrenner Stagetec:** Helmut Benedikt, Thomas Horn, Gerhard Reichart, Wolfgang Salzbrenner **Sandstrahl Bay GmbH:** Martin Bay **santix AG:** Dirk Hoffmann, Esther Kruis, Stefan Schuster, Andrea Stolz, Peter Walden **SCHÄFER GmbH Co. KG:** Jörg Schäfer **Schlegl:** Michael Koch **Schmitt Stumpf Frühauf und Partner:** Thomas Abt, Dieter Benezeder, Florian Böck, Thomas Götzinger, Achim Grünig, Bernd Gschwender, Frank Haake, Christian Hertneck, Andreas Höregott, Helmar Hüning, Ulrich Kauer, Rolf Koppermann, Benedikt Kronenbitter, Matthias Lettau, Anna Levitas, Rainer Linhardt, Apollonia Lorenz, Simone Mank, Helmut Metzler, Michael Nehring, Manfred Pietsch, Hans Reder, Judith Reisert, Kerstin Riebeck, Daniela Ried, Arne Rucks, Manfred Rudolf, Jörg Schaffrath, Victor Schmitt, Holger Schwarz, Ingrid Scippa, Felix Singer, Reiner Tilke, Miklos Tövissy, Ferdinand Tremel, Ernst Wander, Thomas Wolf **Schneider Fassadenplanung GmbH:** Andreas Kapfer, Johann Römer **Schneider GmbH:** Maximilian Schneider **Schöner Boden:** Andreas Hanslmeier, Frank Jäger, Andreas Orlich, Uwe Schmietow, Franz Wimmer, Orhan Yapici **Schottenhammel Catering & Event GmbH:** Christian Schottenhammel **Schunter Beratung Oberfläche:** Erich Schunter **seacon Umformtechnik GmbH:** Martina Gercke, Josef Maurus **section a:** Tulga Beyerle, Katharine Boesch, Christine Haupt-Stummer **SecuFence AG:** Peter Neumann **SECURITAS Sicherheit & Services GmbH & Co. KG:** Michael Alexsandrovskij, Norbert Banas, André´ Bauer, Josef Bayer, Henry Bischoff, Karsten Borngräber, Stephan Dulkies, Henry Fenger, Dirk Großmann, Christian Hartmann, Hans - Georg Heinrich, Manfred Holzner, Sebastian Höttl, Nick Jenne, Güray Karabacak, Rocco Kilz, Jörg Kluge, Hans - Jürgen Lorenz, Peter Lösch, Giuseppe Macrini, Roland Maier, Sven Margies, Anton Mayr, Sebastian Obermann, Jonny Poller, Andreas Scheuermann, Andreas Schlag, Michael Schmidt, Bratislav Stankovic, Sören Stübing, Kurkut Toker, Jakob Tonkuschin, Volker Wagener, Klaus Werner, Michael Wernicke, Mathias Wiese, Dirk Zaremba **SIBC GmbH:** Monika Neubauer, Brigitte Oechsle,

Gabriele Trouillaud, Katharina Wolk **Siegle + Epple:** Walter Dreyer, Franz Hendler, Holger Laib, Katja Lenz, Petra Pfirmann, Sigrid Schneider, Sarah Schweiger, Jörg Schweikert, Holger Staake, Jörg Stoltenberg **SIEMENS AG A&D:** Hans-Jürgen Ringer, Matthias Voss **signa:** Semsi Atici, Brigitte Bischoff, Konstantin Pohlen, Michael Schwinghammer **SiQ GmbH:** Randolf Holl, Wolfgang Kusch, Michael Müller **SLS:** Walter Limbach, Thomas Sauer **SLV München:** Gregor Machura, Martin Schmid **sml grafix:** Susanne Lutz **Softlab GmbH:** Günther Albrecht, Jürgen Brebeck, Andreas Degenhart, Reinhard Fößmeier, Ralf Gebhart, Joachim Hengge, Xiaolei Li, Christian Menk, Ralph Multhammer, Markus Pielmeier, Markus Reiter, Barbara Scheibe, Susanne Scherzinger, Patrick Schirmer, Susanne Völker, Marlies Wohlrab **SOLARWATT AG:** Renè Merdon, Dr. Frank Schneider **Solution 24:** Stefanie Baldauf, Peter Gaßner **Sommer:** Ingo Endl, Richard Hauser, Wolfgang Schaffron, Sven Steller, Renate Trautewein, Mike Weiß **SONUS:** Reinhard Budras, Martin Greis, Joachim Kistner, Frank Näger, Ralf Winkler **SpeiseSyndikat:** Ulrich Stichtmann **SPS Fassadentechnik GmbH:** Alexander Present, Christian Sebastian **Stadler:** Christian Steguweit **Stadtratsfraktion Bündnis90/Die Grünen:** Jutta Koller **Stadtratsfraktion CSU:** Hans Podiuk **Stadtratsfraktion SPD:** Constanze Lindner-Schädlich **Stahlbau Magdeburg:** Evelin Klamke, Dirk Linke, Ralf Luther, Bernd Meinhardt, Bernd Neumann, René Schasse, Bernd von Gebhardi **Stangl:** Klaus Feuerecker, Lars Leupold, Christoph Mentzel, Ulrich Ostermeier, Peter Weidenhöfer **STAWICKI Werbeagentur:** Erich A.M. Stawicki **Stegmüller:** Karl-Heinz Aich, Mario Aigner, Paul Albrecht, Peter Albrecht, Georg Baumgartner, Stefan Birnkammer, Franz Damböck, Michael Erras, Christian Gerhardinger, Konrad Jahrstorfer, Dieter Niemann, Josef Noneder, Robert Noneder, Roland Noneder, Paul Ollmann, Roland Paintmayer, Ingo Scher, Otto Stegmüller sen. **steguweit brand perspektives gmbh:** Jeannine Zschischang **Stöbisch Brandschutz GmbH & Co. KG:** Jörg Nölke **stoiber productions:** Stephan Braun, Sandra Kulbach, Erfried Prenissl, Fritz Stoiber, Christian te Kock **Stork:** Frank Juros, Manfred Müller, Bernd Platte, Joachim Pletziger, Kurt Steins, Wilfried Stork jun., Willi Stork sen **STRABAG AG:** Nobert Brunetti, Robert Liessel **Strömel:** Bernhard Strömel **Studentenwerk München:** Helmut Gierke **Sulzer:** Michail Chiladakis, Heiko Grassmann, Oliver Hahn, Jürgen Schiebler, Dr. Wolfgang Tischer **SunStrom GmbH:** Maik Bermuske, Sten Birnbaum, Marko Grimm, Wilhelm Günther, Rene Hauschild, Olaf Jannaschk, Wolfgang Junge, Lutz Kaden, Heiko Karisch, Peter Kästner, Jens Kleen, Marcel Kronmüller, Karel Kubicki, Reiner Matthees, Matthias Modrey, Mirko Pfeiffer, Daniel Priem, Patrick Schädlich, Florian Schweizer, Adrien Söhnel, Stephan Streit, Steffen Stürzkober, Hauke Willamowski, Norbert Zerlik **Susanne Schmid Beratung & Training:** Susanne Schmid **SZG-Engineering:** Rüdiger Schidzig **TAW:** Holger Klein, Kay-Uwe Mundt, Christian Wehmeyer, Thomas A. Weisse **Taxi-München eG:** Thomas Kroker **TEAM KONZEPT Ladenbau & Projektservice GmbH:** Mathias Schmidt **TEAM KONZEPT Manufacture & Planning:** Marcus Schmidt **team m & m Werbeagentur:** Jan Steinocher **The English Institut:** Frank Steele **The Ritz Carlton Catering:** Jörg Tüttelmann **theapro:** Reinhold Daberto, Sebastian Fenk, Jörg Lilleike, Ralph Preller, Markus Pusch, Frank Schöpf, Benito Seravalle, Smith Tom, Ulrich Zimmermann **THEMATA - Freizeit-und Erlebniswelten Services:** Norbert Altenhöner, Sabine Friedrich **ThyssenKruppSchulte:** Dietmar Schwarz, Silvia Zetsche **Ticket.International:** Harald Elsen, Martin Koreis, Robert Weyrauch **T-Mobile:** Frank Buchholz, Peter Müller **Top:** Jozef Bachenek, Stanislaw Bartosinski, Christian Bartz, Jacek Borunsinski, J. Krzysztof Dudek, Leszek Fatalski, Daniel Grezelka, Leszek Jamrotz, Kukasz Kacorowski, Boguslaw Knez, Frank Köhler, Marian Konieczke, Waldimar Matejka, Kazimierz Mglosiek, Pawel Opatowicz, Harald Pedolzky, Eugeniusz Pizystape, Dariusz Potapowicz, Idojciech Raszeja, Andrzej Rutkowski, Paul Siebert, Stefan Staska, Artur Szmajda, Peter Ullrich, Jan Wiaderniy, Czeskali Wojfas, Zygmunt Zalewski, Marian Zybura **TOP Textilpflege:** Waltraud Heunisch **top Zulassungsservice GmbH:** Georg Escoda **Tourismusamt München:** Georg Ansmann, Astrid Gansen, Rupert Geiger, Jörg Lutz, Hedda Manhard, Melanie Reif, Gertrud Schaller, Nicola Seeger, Claudia Weidenkopf, Dr. Gabriele Weishäupl, Ralf Zednik **Tourismusverband München-Oberbayern:** Christine Lichtenauer **Transport Service Beitinger GmbH & Co. KG:** Edwin Beitinger **TRUST Promotion GmbH:** Anke Langhardt, Meike Leuchtner **T-Systems ITS GmbH:** Attila Gallaire, Ralf Kennerknecht, Silke Mirwa, Heiko Schrader, Dr. Stefan Schwanenberg **TVS:** Röger Carsten **Typico:** Herlinde Böhler, Helmut Cavegn, Jürgen Dürnberger, Markus Graz, Norbert Graz, Walter Klocker, Birgit Stix, Theo Sulea **Ventus:** Gerard Mulder **Verlagsagentur Heyne:** Friederike Heyne **via management consulting GmbH:** Dr. Dieter Knon **vianova company:** Peter Apel, Christian Borchert, Gerd Engelbart, Carmen Krüger **Vires:** Marius Dupuis **Vitra Design Museum:** Irmtraud Hager **Vokal:** Jürgen Roche **Vollert Anlagenbau GmbH + Co. KG:** Jochen Keinath, Henry Schulze, Jürgen Streit **W & P Publipress:** Wilfried Tichy, Klaus Wäschle **Waagner Biro:** Heinz Bauer, Alois Fürthaler, Leopold Hülber, Georg Krickl, Peter Neubauer, Harald Pöschel, Thomas Schmädeke, Alfred Trautner **Wagner GmbH:** Christian Dupier, Tobias Grossmann, Frank Hellrung, Sören Schiller, Marion Senkel, Vladimir Tietz **Walkenhorst Osnabrück GmbH:** Henry Walkenhorst **WALO Bertschinger AG, Zürich:** Antonio Antunes, Paulo Barroca, Marcello Bonadei, Manuel Cardoso Sousa, Aurelio Conçalves, Luis Da Costa, Filipe Da Cunha, Joaquim Da Cunha, José Da Fonseca, Claudio Da Silva, Marco Da Silva, Casimiro De Sousa, Correlo Antonio De Sousa, José Pedro De Sousa, Luis De Sousa, Ricardo Fernandes, Celestino Ferreira, Antonio Gonçalves, Carlos Gonçalves, Luis Manuel Machado, Manuel Matos, Hanspeter Merz, Jorge Oliveira, Ricardo Pereira, Manuel Rocha, Manuel Sampaio, Marco Soares, Paulo Vieira, Carsten Weber, Ramon Zwahlen **WALTER KNOLL AG & Co. KG:** Daniel Eckes **Wampfler AG:** Guido Ahlfeld, Ulrich Günther, Eberhard Vonhof **WashTec Cleaning Technology GmbH:** Jochen Schraff, Andreas Thoma **Werbetechnik Deger GmbH:** Franz Deger, Helmut Loschka **Werk5 Mangold Helmer GmbH:** Gunnar Bloss, Hauke Helmer, Ulrich Mangold **Wilms GmbH:** Thomas Buchholz, Nicolai Eichwald, Bilal Hasan, Franz Ignatz, Rico Illing, Waldemar Imgrund, Adam Keterling, Valentin Keterling, Egon Lassel, Markus Meier, Conny Michel, Gerd Müller, Matthias Müller, Andreas Rode, Hamit Savci, Roger Tauschisky, Sven Thormann, Josef Weickert, Rudi Wellmann, Peter Wilms, Thomas Wilms **Winkelsesser Fliesen - Estriche GmbH:** Joachim Fischer, Roland Parsch, Günter Winkelsesser **Wöhr:** Joachim Kugler **xmobil:** Christian Grübl **ZARGES:** Michael Habersetzer, Stefan Pfleger, Rainer Riedl, Helmut Schwarz **Zeichen & Wunder GmbH:** Irmgard Hesse, Petra Morcher, Max Rauscher, Patrick von Hausen **Zeiler-Technik:** Christian Blüml, Johannes Brandner, Hans Dobosch, Andreas Heilingbrunner, Stefan Hirschauer, Klaus Kothe, Stefan Kroiß, Alfred Leitl, Manfred Rammonat, Anton Rott, Hans Zeiler, Jürgen Zinßmeister **Zilch - Müller - Hennecke:** Yvonne Giese, Angelika Hillebrand, Peter Lenz, Dr. André Müller, Wolfgang Niedermeier, Arnd Paus, Dr. Erwin Penka, Nicolai Pfitzenmeier, Daniele Salvatore, Karl Schwindl, Stefan Summerer, Prof. Dr. Konrad Zilch **zweiB GmbH, audiovisual Eventengineering:** Tammo Buhren **Sowie:** Gernot Brauer, Michael Cantana, Sibilni Codor, Melanie Girdlestone, Karl-Heinz Kieltsch, Christopher La Bonté, Stephan Matheiowetz, Morssaov Mustafa, Ali Nasim, Wolfgang Norkauer, Edgar Scherl, Jürgen Strasser

Wir danken allen, die am Projekt beteiligt waren und die bei der Entstehung der BMW Welt mitgewirkt haben. Auch jenen, deren Namen wir nicht in Erfahrung bringen konnten. We wish to thank all who participated in this project, and those who contributed to the realization of the BMW Welt, as well as all those whose names we were unable to ascertain.

Bildnachweis _ picture credits: S. 14-17 Hubertus Hamm, S. 18 Coop Himmelb(l)au, Wien, S. 21/25 BMW AG, S. 29-33 BMW AG, S. 37 BMW AG, Marcus Buck, BMW AG, S. 38 BMW AG, S. 41 BMW AG, Designworks USA, S. 42 BMW AG, S. 45 BMW AG, S. 47 Coop Himmelb(l)au, Wien, S. 51-55 [phase eins], Berlin, S. 56-64 Coop Himmelb(l)au, Wien, BMW AG, S. 69 Coop Himmelb(l)au, Wien, BMW AG, S. 70-74 Marcus Buck, S. 77-104 Marcus Buck, S. 107 Hubertus Hamm, S. 120-202 Hubertus Hamm, S. 203 Studio Hamm: Jan Schünke, S. 204-241 Hubertus Hamm, S. 242 BMW AG, Marcus Buck, S. 243 Marcus Buck

Unserer besonderer Dank gilt _ Our special thanks to:
dem BMW Historischen Archiv, dem BMW Group MediaPool, Helmut Pöschl, Dr. Florian Triebel,
Dr. Caroline Schulenburg, Wolfram Greiner, Doris Lönner, Andreas Hemmerle, Elisabeth von Mengden,
Andreas Hocke, Alexander Hildebrandt, Uwe Mahla, Gerhard Menz, Claudia Wieshuber, Lars Freisinger,
Edith Julia Rom, Jos-Philip Ostendorf, Michaela Gilg, dem Leitungsteam und den Mitarbeiterinnen und
Mitarbeitern der BMW Welt sowie den Mitarbeiterinnen und Mitarbeitern der BMW Group, die uns bei den
Recherchen, der Texterstellung, den Fotoshootings und der Bildauswahl unterstützt haben.

Herausgeber _ Publisher	BMW AG, BMW Welt, München
Projektleitung BMW _ Project management BMW	Roman Diehl, Dr. Sibylle Beate Waegner
Autor _ Author	Gernot Brauer
Projektleitung Agentur _ Project management agency	Friederike Heyne Verlagsagentur GmbH, Hamburg
Art Direktion _ Art direction	Bettina Oswald
Lektorat _ Chief editor	Sandra-Kathrin Buck
Redaktion _ Editorial work	Manuela Kießl
Fotografen _ Photographers	Hubertus Hamm, Marcus Buck
Fotoarchiv _ Photo archives	BMW AG: BMW Historisches Archiv,
	BMW Group MediaPool, BMW PressClub
Übersetzung _ Translation	Werkstatt München, Jon Smale
DTP und Produktion _ DTP and production	Hauptmann & Kompanie Werbeagentur,
	München - Zürich, Cornelia Hepting
Postproduktion _ Post production	Delta E GmbH
Druck und Bindung _ Printing and binding	Zanardi Group, Italy
Schutzumschlag _ Jacket Design	© Hubertus Hamm
Cover Illustration _ Cover Illustration	© Coop Himmelb(l)au, Wien

© 2008 teNeues Verlag GmbH + Co.KG, Kempen

Picture and text rights reserved for all countries.
No part of this publication may be reproduced
in any manner whatsoever. All rights reserved.

Published by teNeues Publishing Group

teNeues Verlag GmbH + Co. KG
Am Selder 37
47906 Kempen, Germany
Phone: 0049-(0)2152-916-0
Fax: 0049-(0)2152-916-111
e-mail: books@teneues.de

Press department: arehn@teneues.de
Phone: 0049-(0)2152-916-202

teNeues Publishing Company
16 West 22nd Street
New York, NY 10010, USA
Phone: 001-212-627-9090
Fax: 001-212-627-9511

teNeues Publishing UK Ltd.
P.O. Box 402
West Byfleet, KT14 7ZF, Great Britain
Phone: 0044-(0)1932-40 35 09
Fax: 0044-(0)1932-40 35 14

teNeues France S.A.R.L.
93, rue Bannier
45000 Orléans, France
Phone: 0033-(0)2-38 54 10 71
Fax: 0033-(0)2-38 62 53 40

www.teneues.com

While we strive for utmost precision in every detail,
we cannot be held responsible for any inaccuracies,
neither for any subsequent loss or damage arising.

Bibliographic information published by Die Deutsche
Bibliothek. Die Deutsche Bibliothek lists this publication
in the Deutsche Nationalbibliografie; detailed bibliographic data is available in the Internet at http://dnb.ddb.de.

ISBN: 978-3-8327-9231-2
Printed in Italy

teNeues Publishing Group
Kempen
Düsseldorf
Hamburg
London
Madrid
Milan
Munich
New York
Paris

teNeues